Hans-Liudger Dienel, Heike Walk, Angela Jain, Sabine Schröder,
Bhaskar Poldas, Saira Alam, Shilpa Deekshith, Rama Rao

Constraints and Opportunities for the Development of Communication and Participation Strategies

Analysis for a political dialogue on climate friendly city development

Emerging megacities
Dicussion Papers
Edited by Konrad Hagedorn, Christine Werthmann, Dimitrios Zikos, Ramesh Chennamaneni

Humboldt-Universität zu Berlin
Department of Agricultural Economics
Division of Resource Economics
Philippstr. 13, House 12
10115 Berlin

Tel.: +49 (0)30 2093 6305
Fax: +49 (0)30 2093 6497
www.agrar.hu-berlin.de/struktur/institute/wisola/fg/ress
www.sustainable-hyderabad.de

Contact: emerging.megacities@hu-berlin.de

The emerging megacities discussion papers are available at:
www.eh-verlag.de

ISSN print edition 2193-6927

Emerging megacities Discussion Papers are prepared by researchers working on topics in the realm of sustainable development in Megacities of Tomorrow, a research priority by the German Ministry of Education and Research (BMBF). The papers have been peer-reviewed by a board of external reviewers.
Views and opinions expressed do not necessarily represent those of the Division of Resource Economics.
Comments are highly welcome and should be sent directly to the authors.
We welcome contributions on any topics related to Megacities of Tomorrow. Further information on the submission procedure is given at:
www.sustainable-hyderabad.de/emerging-megacities

Dienel, Hans-Liudger; Walk, Heike; Jain, Angela; Schröder, Sabine; Poldas, Bhaskar; Alam, Saira; Deekshith, Shilpa; Rao, Rama

Constraints and Opportunities for the Development of Communication and Participation Strategies
Analysis for a political dialogue on climate friendly city development

Emerging megacities Discussion Papers, Volume 2/2009

ISBN/EAN: 978-3-86741-814-0
First published in 2012 by Europaeischer Hochschulverlag GmbH & Co KG, Bremen, Germany.

© Europaeischer Hochschulverlag GmbH & Co KG, Fahrenheitstr. 1, D-28359 Bremen (www.eh-verlag.de). All rights reserved.

Cover: Photo "Metropolis", ferendus (flickr). Creative Commons License

No part of this publication may be reproduced or transmitted, in any form or by any means, electronic, mechanical, photocopying, recording or otherwise, or stored in any retrieval system of nay nature, without the written permission of the copyright holder and the publisher, application for which shall be made to the publisher.

EHV

Constraints and Opportunities for the Development of Communication and Participation Strategies

Analysis for a political dialogue on climate friendly city development

Hans-Liudger Dienel[*], Heike Walk[†], Angela Jain[‡,*], Sabine Schröder[*], Bhaskar Poldas[*], Saira Alam[*], Shilpa Deckshith[§], Rama Rao[¶]

May 2009

Abstract

The background analysis focuses mainly on chances for civil society participation, its democratic legitimacy and the existing forms and experiences of civil society participation, as well as constraints to participation and access to information. Furthermore, relevant stakeholders are identified with a focus on civil society organisations in Hyderabad, which are active in the field of climate protection, energy, sustainability, and environment, and their goals, activities, strengths and weaknesses, networks and specific needs described. On the basis of the stakeholder analysis, multiplicators within civil society that are relevant to the project's areas, can be identified for participative processes with other WPs. Based on these findings and in an iterative process to test strategies, the participation strategies can be adapted to the local, cultural and civil society context in Hyderabad.

Key words: *citizens participation, civil society, stakeholder dialogue, city development, Hyderabad, India*

---

[*] nexus - Institute for Cooperation Management and Interdisciplinary Research GmbH, Otto-Suhr-Allee 59, Berlin
[†] Centre for Technology and Society, Hardenbergstr. 16-18, 10623 Berlin
[‡] Corresponding author. Tel.: +49 30 3180 5466. Email: jain@nexusinstitut.de
[§] Osmania University, Hyderabad
[¶] Center for World Solidarity, Hyderabad

1 Introduction

Participative and communicative methods are essential to create and increase awareness for the set of problems associated to climate change and for mitigation- and adaptation strategies among affected stakeholders. It is likewise essential, to integrate the local knowledge and the needs of the affected groups in developing these strategies and to activate the stakeholders to take self-initiative. The discussion on the reasons and consequences of climate change is taking place at different levels today, but is only marginally reaching the population. To ensure a sustainable growth process for the megacity Hyderabad there is a need for close co-operation between stakeholders of civil society, economy, science and government in developing political strategies. The issue of 'Climate Change and Energy Efficiency' demands new forms and ways of communication and participation. These consist in an intensive dialogue and discussion on the reasons and consequences of climate change, which is not only directed at political solutions, but also includes possibilities of self-action in daily routines. Thus, communication and participation strategies aim, on the one hand, at the dialogue and cooperation between the different stakeholders of all levels (civil society, business, science and government), and, on the other hand, on the possibilities for fostering low-emission lifestyles at the individual level of every citizen.

In this background study the framework for a political dialogue on climate friendly, energy efficient city development is analysed. The analysis addresses the discourse on climate change in India and the public awareness of the issue. Furthermore, it demonstrates how issue-framing is relevant for mobilising and activating citizens for the cause of environment and climate change. Furthermore, it analyses the state of civil society in India and its chances for participation, its democratic legitimacy and the existing forms and experiences of participation in India, as well as constraints to participation and access to information.

The assignment is to foster stakeholder dialogue and citizen participation and to involve stakeholders and citizens in the activities and pilot projects of the overall project. Therefore, relevant stakeholders are identified in this analysis. The focus of the stakeholder analysis is on the civil society sector and thus, relevant civil society organisations in Hyderabad, which are active in the fields of research of the project (climate change, energy, sustainability, and environment) and their goals, activities, strengths and weaknesses, networks and specific needs are identified and described. On the basis of this analysis, multipliers within civil society can be identified for participative processes. Based on the findings of this background study and in an iterative process to test strategies, participation and communication strategies can be adapted to the local context in Hyderabad.

2 Communicating Environment and Climate Change in India

2.1 The Discourse on Climate Change in India

Climate change in India is often perceived – in academic and popular discourse alike – as a "global" challenge, a threat "beyond borders". India and other developing countries feel strongly that they are not responsible for climate change. This is emphasised through the fact that in the intergovernmental climate negotiations India has consistently argued against greenhouse gas mitigation commitments for developing countries. Though India is resisting calls by developed countries to take on specific targets for the reduction of its Greenhouse Gas emissions, the Indian government has declared that even as it pursues its social and economic development objectives, it will not allow its per capita GHG emissions to exceed the average per capita emissions of the developed countries. India is a country, which is and will continue to be severely impacted by climate change, precisely at a time when it is confronted with huge development imperatives. India believes that addressing climate change, especially through investment in renewable energies, could create new jobs and spur technology innovation.

The discourse on climate change in India has tended to be obscured by technical and scientific issues. Much of climate change discussion has revolved around technicalities such as carbon emissions. For the most part, the jargon used is difficult to understand by those who are not scientists. In 2008, India has announced a National Action Plan on Climate Change (NAPCC), which incorporates its vision of sustainable development (with eight national missions) and the steps it must take to realise it.[1] Unfortunately, there is no statement of a baseline of current emissions and projected trajectory under a business-as-usual scenario, against which targets are set or achievements over and above the normal trend could be assessed. There is also no overarching target or goal that knits NAPCC together. India has an Energy Conservation Act under which it has identified nine energy intensive industries for observance of mandatory energy efficiency standards. The NAPCC also has a National Mission on Improving Energy Efficiency.

---

[1] http://pmindia.nic.in/Pg01-52.pdf.

In the 2009 elections India's main political parties are offering environment plans in their manifestos for the first time, but the chances of climate policies to limit emissions in the future seem to be slim, because of the low priority they get from decision-makers. The lack of awareness contrasts sharply with the fact that India is among the countries most at risk from climate change. In India's vast countryside, climate change concerns are hardly existent, even as global warming begins to leave an indelible mark on the lives of the poor. The concern for environmental problems in India is relatively new and more or less remains restricted to a few individuals. The awareness for environmental protection at the policy level is mostly induced by donors, and at the grassroots level it is due to the efforts of a few individuals and NGOs.

However, according to newer international public opinion polls the picture of environmental awareness is more contradictory. While a study by the BBC (2007) showed that the Indian public displayed little awareness of global warming or climate change compared to other countries and the figures for thinking that it is necessary to take major steps soon were below average[2], there seems to be a high awareness about climate change and the need to protect the environment according to a climate confidence study published in 2008 by the multinational firm HSBC (Hong Kong and Shanghai Banking Corporation). In the study 9,000 consumers in nine major economies including the US, China, Germany and India were polled. Among the nine countries, 60 % of respondents in India showed great concern for the problem of climate change as against 32 % in the US and 26 % in Germany.[3] Similar results were presented in the Human Development Report 2007/2008. This suggests that the awareness of climate change and the understanding that steps have to be taken is growing in India.

Especially India's youth seems to be aware of the set of problems of climate change and is confident that human activism can make a change. In 2008, Hyderabad celebrated a momentous occasion, as the nation's first Youth Summit on Climate Change took place, organised by the Indian Youth Climate Network. Young people from all over India showed that they have a strong vested interest in helping to bring climate change under control because they will otherwise have to live with its increasingly severe consequences over the coming decades. In June 2009, the Youth Summit on Climate Change will again take place in Hyderabad. It is planned to formulate a Hyderabad Youth Charter on Climate Change that shall reflect the efforts of the Indian youth concerning development and sustainability in regard to climate change. Furthermore, a

---

[2] BBC (2007)
[3] HSBC (2008)

discourse on the implementation of practices and ideas concerning mitigation strategies across Hyderabad as well as a network of youth and government bodies is going to be established.[4]

In our understanding, the lack of climate change awareness is mainly a matter of issue-framing, i.e. of linking the issue of climate change to matters of concern to the people, e.g. livelihood and development. Many studies show that, if climate change is framed exclusively as an isolated scientific matter, very few people will be interested, especially if facing pressing everyday needs.[5] On the other hand, many other studies show that climate change, if framed as a matter of affecting people's livelihoods in concrete ways, is in fact by no means a luxury concern of affluent and well educated middle-class members of developed countries.[6] This argument can be proven by the next chapter, describing different environmental movements in India and their success according to their issue-framing and communication strategies.

2.2 Communicating the Environment – Environmental Movements in India

In the absence of awareness and concern for environment among large parts of the population, the environmental aspects do not build the basis of most movements. Some movements from the past are portrayed today as ecological or environmental, because they widened their focus from basic survival needs of affected people to ecological concerns. Basically, some of these movements were established to ensure the survival of local people, as ecological aspects are directly linked with the survival of peasants, who depend on natural resources. Later on, their focus was diversified to include ecological concerns.

Environmental movements in India, therefore, are not necessarily for the 'green' or 'clean' earth or for saving endangered species as in the west, but for the very survival of the local poor.[7] Interestingly, the success of the movement is often linked with its popularity rather than the importance of the issue.

The matter of issue-framing of environmental concerns and the reasons for the popularity/success or failure of movements with ecological concerns is discussed in detail by Reddy (1997): The Chipko (hugging the trees) Movement in the central Himalayan re-

---

[4] Information gathered from initiatives website: www.iycn.in/about.htm.
[5] Weber (2008)
[6] WWF-India (2006)
[7] Rao (1994)

gion in the early 1970s and the movements against building major dams on rivers – Tehri Dam in Garhwal region in North India, Silent Valley Project in Kerala and Narmada Valley Project in Central India – are some examples.

2.2.1 The Chipko Movement

The origin of modern environmentalism and environmental movements in India can be ascribed to the Chipko movement in the early 1970s, which was launched to protect the Himalayan forests from destruction. Although it has its' roots in the pre-independence days, Chipko movement in fact started in the year 1973.[8] The forest department had refused to allot ash trees to a local co-operative organisation to make agricultural tools and allotted them instead to a private company to produce sport equipment. This triggered the fight of the villagers in the region against the injustice done. At the beginning, they tried in vain to stop the company from felling trees by lying in front of timber trucks, burning resin and timber depots. When these methods failed, one of the leaders, Chandi Prasad Bhat, suggested embracing the trees and thus, Chipko movement was born. Chipko has kindled the environmental aspects of development and gave rise to numerous conflicts and protests over natural resources and ecological issues. However, none of the following forest based movements attracted the same public support as Chipko. This can be attributed to three important aspects. Firstly, the movement was closely linked to people's livelihood. Chipko movement did not only address the felling of trees but also formulated several demands to ameliorate local people's livelihood. In addition to that, Chipko achieved to attract the support of many women with its accompanying anti-alcohol campaign. Secondly, Chipko has strictly adhered to the Ghandian principle of non-violence. Thirdly, the perception of the leaders like Shri Sunderlal Bahuguna as being sincere and simple and their access to national leaders like Mrs. Indira Gandhi and other politicians and officials also helped to the success of the movement to a large extent. It is interesting to note that in the later stages, when Chipko ceased to go beyond environmental concerns, i.e. limiting itself

---

[8] The Chipko movement is actually rooted in the Bishnoi community in Rajasthan, who practiced environmental conservation as part of their religious duty. This small community, an offspring of Hinduism founded in the 15th century by Guru Maharaj Jambaji, had a codex of 29 principles, of which one was not to fell green trees. When in the 18th century the King of Jodhpur ordered his soldiers to get timber from the Bishnoi area for his palace, the Bishnoi women protested against the felling of the trees by encircling them with their bodies. However, the soldiers killed the women and felled the trees. When the King came to know of this event he ordered his soldiers back and granted the Bishnois state protection for their beliefs (Srivastava 2006 and Dwivedi 2000).

to protecting and conserving trees, problems started to surface and the movement lost support.

2.2.2 The Tehri Dam, Silent Valley and Narmada Valley Movements

The other popular movements of importance in India, which have environmental protection as one of their objectives, relate to major dams. Notable among them are Tehri Dam, Silent Valley and Narmada Valley Projects. The movement against building Tehri Dam organised by the committee, Tehri Bandh Virodhi Sangarshan Samithi, focussed on environmental issues. The two major objections concerning environment they raised were seismic sensitivity of the region and submergence of forest areas along with Tehri town. Despite being supported by prominent leaders the movement failed to gain enough support and eventually the Dam was constructed.

The environmental movement against the Silent Valley hydro electric project in Kerala was successful, as the project was eventually abandoned. The movement was organised by the council Kerala Sastra Sahitya Parishat (KSSP) in collaboration with wild life conservationists. No local people were involved in the movement, though, as there was no displacement of people due to the proposed project. It was fought primarily on grounds of the environment and predominantly at the intellectual level. The major concerns of this movement were the adverse environmental impact on Silent Valley, one of the last surviving natural tropical forests in India and protecting a rare breed of monkey. It received active support from international organisations like World Wildlife Fund and the International Union for the Conservation of Nature and Natural Resources. But its ultimate success is attributed to the initiative of the then Prime Minister Mrs. Indira Gandhi.

The Narmada Bacho Andolan (Save Narmada Agitation) Movement, which fought against building the Narmada River Valley Dam was the most popular movement in the environmental history of India. It was started in the 1970s and gained momentum in 1980s. The issue of human rights was the basis for this movement. It fought for the rehabilitation of the people displaced by the dam. It gained public attention with the mobilisation and organisation of the affected local people, mostly tribals, and the eminent social workers like Baba Amte, Sunderlal Bahuguna and Medha Patkar joining the movement. Its major success was to convince the World Bank, which funded the project, to withdraw its support for it. Nevertheless, the movement failed as the Supreme Court of India decided in favour of the Government and subsequently the dam was built.

2.2.3 Issue-Framing of the movements' aims

Taking a closer look at the different movements, it can be noticed that movements with fast-changing and multiple objectives are capable to sustain for longer periods and more successful. The Chipko movement had wide ranging objectives such as, protecting the livelihoods of peasants, an anti-liquor campaign, greening the hills in a sustainable fashion, etc. which have changed over time. Besides these, its popularity and success are attributed to its long history, committed leaders and their stature at local and national level. When it started to limit its objectives to environmental issues, Chipko lost its popularity.

Narmada movement, apart from addressing different issues, followed different strategies to influence national and international audiences by explaining things from one point of view to the human rights activists, and from another to the environmental groups. Like Chipko, it started with addressing the problems of livelihood of local tribals, traversed into human rights issues and at the same time focused on environmental concerns while suggesting an alternative development paradigm. Interestingly, the strategy of the leadership has been to address all these dimensions simultaneously in an effective manner. Its mass base, the dam affected tribal communities, were homogeneous, had no modern influence and hence were easier to be organised.

Meanwhile, the Bhopal gas tragedy, where about 2,500 people lost their lives while thousands became permanently disabled, did not have these qualities of a mass movement. It was a sudden tragedy dawned upon a heterogeneous urban community. Through the Bhopal Act, passed in March 1985, the Government of India consolidated all claims arising out of the disaster and made the government the only competent authority to represent the victims. Thus, there was no possibility to mobilise people around the issue of livelihood and link it to environment. The issue has always been the compensation but never the future policy on environmentally dangerous industries. It seems therefore, that environmental issues per se do not have the potential to draw mass attraction. There are many other examples in India, where important environmental issues are not tackled by environmentalists. There are hardly any movements that concern urban or industrial pollution.[9]

A similar result could be noticed while implementing the pilot projects within the Megacity Project "Sustainable Hyderabad". During the conference on "Hyderabad Citizens Charter for Sustainable Urban Transport" it was seen that the traffic problem is not perceived primarily as an environmental or energy problem, but rather as a safety

---

[9] see Reddy (1997)

(e.g. low safety for pedestrians, too many accidents) and time problem (traffic jams and long commuting times).

Nevertheless, according to recent international public opinion polls there seems to be a growing awareness about the need to protect the environment and to fight climate change which was shown in the climate confidence study by HSBC mentioned earlier.

The above discussion shows that methods of awareness raising and activating citizens for climate and energy related problems have to link aspects which are important to the people and affect their daily lives to the necessity of energy efficiency and mitigation. Furthermore, the aspects of climate protection and energy-efficiency have to be linked to socioeconomic development issues in general. This also implies that an ecocentric approach (borrowed from western movements) may not suit to developing countries, as the main concerns here continue to be basic needs. Hence, the approach in India ought to be different from that of the western countries.

3 Civil Society in India

During the last two decades the idea of civil society has gained significance in social sciences and political policy. Although there are many differing concepts of civil society, civil society can be defined as the sphere of organisations in the space between the state and the household or family/kinship, which are voluntary in nature and have significant autonomy from the state. According to Harriss (2005) "it also refers to the space in which people can come together in a way that is not dictated by the state or family or kinship, where they can debate and engage in public affairs."[10]

A series of exemplary definitions of civil society from European eyes (Hegel, Gramsci, Marx, Foucault) have been analysed, followed by discussions of Indian sociologists (Rajini Kothari, André Béteille, Dipankar Gupta, Partha Chatterjee, and others). Following these, it seems to be necessary to take a cosmopolitan approach towards civil society, which distances itself from eurocentrism and seeks an Indian modernism and a specifically Indian definition of civil society.[11] The concept of civil society for India has to be extended in a way that allows integrating caste councils and caste associations, as these institutions – despite their particular ascribed relations – represent an area of civic engagement and participatory decision-making and form a forum for solidarity and a civic culture of discussion and debate.[12]

---

[10] Harriss (2005), p. 3
[11] Randeria, Shalini (2004), p. 156
[12] ibid.

According to Kailash Mishra (2002), civil society participation is rooted in Indian traditions. Vedic hymns describe egalitarian and democratic norms of their society, for example people's assemblies like Vidath, Sabha and Samiti. Vidath was a general reunion of the whole community, which had redistributive functions. Sabhas were bodies of village elders who assisted the rulers. Samiti was a general assembly in which all the members of a community participated and elected the ruler. Remarkably, in all these assemblies women participated as well as men. Furthermore, all the Vedic assemblies' decisions were taken on the basis of consensus only. In the Vedic hymns, voluntary social work is mentioned, as well.

Educational work and social involvement are also part of the Brahmin (highest caste of Priests) ideals. Furthermore, the tradition of self-help builds on Christian missionaries who were very engaged in voluntary social work especially in Southern India. The Missionaries of Charities of Mother Theresa in Calcutta have become famous all over the world.

In modern times the Ghandian philosophy and his way of life have given a new rise to social engagement. Until today, many voluntary workers see themselves as working in the tradition of Ghandi, especially in the western states of Gujarat, Rajasthan, Madhya Pradesh and Maharashtra.[13]

Through organisations such as PRIA (Participators Research in Asia) in Delhi and PAC (Public Affairs Centre) in Bangalore many Indian activists have made contributions to thinking and practicing on the role of civil society. However, there is little empirical research on the structure and character of the existing civil society in India.[14]

The organisations of civil society in India can take different forms, which include associations and their umbrella bodies, trade unions, foundations, consumer organisations, Non Governmental Organisations (NGOs) and Community-Based Organisations (CBOs), religious organisations delivering welfare services, interest groups, self-help groups, neighbourhood action committees, residents welfare associations, caste councils etc. Therefore, any people's association or organisation can be referred to as a Civil Society Organisation (CSO)[15]. These can mobilise and work for a specific cause, engage in social welfare activities or represent the needs and interests of a certain community. The civil society organisations can be divided in different levels. At the base level, there are Community Based Organisations, like residents' welfare associations, women's associations or slum dwellers associations, which are rooted within a geographically defined

---

[13] Randeria, Shalini (2004)
[14] Harriss (2005)
[15] CGG (2006)

community and address the immediate problems of their community. They are thus directly linked to the citizens. Furthermore, there are more formal or structured CSOs operating at local, state or national level. They often work to benefit others and specialise in certain topics, e.g. environmental organisations. NGOs, as opposed to CBOs, are mostly referred to as organisations that have professional staff, receive funds and are nationally and internationally linked. Umbrella organisations, thematic networks and constituted platforms can be seen as a further level of civil society.

In his study on civil society in Chennai Harriss (2005) states that especially and increasingly members of the Indian middle-class[16] are engaging in CSOs and describe themselves increasingly as 'activists'. According to him "it seems possible that as middle-class people have either failed to take on leadership roles in the sphere of political society, or have vacated that sphere–as they have according to the electoral studies which have demonstrated their declining political participation–so they have increasingly found in civil society the domain for their self-assertion." This implies that they have given up on the political sphere in order to engage in civil society activism, and in doing so de-valorise party political activity.

In India a dynamic and diversified civil society has evolved during the last two decades. There is a growing involvement of civil society in developing long-term and replicable social and economic development initiatives.[17] Through participative social and development work, CSOs have managed to open up new possibilities for minorities and backward classes to alleviate their poverty and enhance their livelihood, where governmental programs have failed to reach the great number of under-privileged in a segmented society.[18] While CSO activities were for a long time mainly concerned with issues of development, poverty alleviation and advocating for the poor and discriminated, in recent years issues of environment have gained greater importance.

4 Institutional Framework for Participation in India

India's still youthful democracy was formed in 1947, when the country was emancipated from colonial British rule. India's struggle for freedom was firmly rooted in the desire for popular government; and, along with its hard-won independence, law and policy making

---

[16] The term 'middle-class' does not quite fit in the Indian context, as the Indian middle-class does not represent the broad 'middle' of society. Still the term is widely used in India.
[17] CGG (2006)
[18] Kuhn (2006)

was finally in the hands of the Indians themselves. Political participation in India has changed in many ways since then:

> *New social groups have entered the political arena and begun to use their political re-sources to shape the political process. Scheduled Castes and Scheduled Tribes, previously excluded from politics because of their position at the bottom of India's social hierarchy, have begun to take full advantage of the opportunities presented by India's democracy. Women and environmentalists constitute new political categories that transcend traditional distinctions.*[19]

However, India has also seen major troubles in realising a truly representative and transparent governance structure, despite heavy lip service by Indian authorities to participatory governance and its benefits in recent years.

4.1 Attempts at Decentralised Democracy

Attempts at creating a decentralised India have been a relatively recent phenomenon; before the 73rd and 74th constitutional amendments of 1993, municipal and local level elected representation did not exist. These two amendments respectively created rural (panchayats, 73rd amendment) and urban (nagarapalikas, 74th amendment) local-level authorities. Additionally, and equally important, these amendments mandated a sort of positive discrimination, which reserved elected posts for women and members of the untouchable and "other backward classes", in attempts to have a more equitable representation of the population in government than had previously been the case.[20] However, it was only in 1997 that one half of India's states had, in accordance with these two amendments, actually devolved considerable powers upon and created elected offices at the local and municipal levels, such as Andhra Pradesh's creation of the Municipal Corporation of Hyderabad, which is now the Greater Hyderabad Municipal Corporation (GHMC, the city's government).[21] It is noteworthy that in devolving these powers, new local level governments are currently seen and treated not as truly independent bodies, but rather as an extension of the state from which they received their powers. For example, although a number of important responsibilities were constitutionally mandated to be transferred to these newly created bodies, the central government has given states an extremely flexible timetable to complete this task; in Andhra Pradesh, many issues

---

[19] Heitzmann / Worden (1995)
[20] Sharma (2002)
[21] Dahiya, Bharat (2000)

which one would consider very local in nature were not actually handed over to the municipal level until 2004.

While there has been quite a progress in creating Panchayati Raj institutions in rural areas according to the 73rd Amendment – although there are still enormous challenges in implementing legal provisions – such leadership is sorely lacking in urban decentralisation. So far, only the states of Kerala and West Bengal have respected the spirit of it. Andhra Pradesh has only introduced Zonal Committees of every ten corporators, so far.

The 74th Amendment also made constitutional provision for Ward Committees under the Municipal Corporation. Each Ward Committee comprises of an elected counsellor of the ward with residents of the ward as members. The Ward Committee deals with issues which directly concern the residents of that ward. In practice, Ward Committees in their current form have been proved ineffective as the group they represent is too large. Moreover, they have no powers or funds. Thus, a new community participation law originally known as Nagara Raj Bill 2004 is necessary to create institutionalised space for citizen participation. According to this bill wards need to be further divided into Area Sabhas, which may consist of two or more contiguous polling booths. Each Area Sabha elects one member for the Ward Committee. The Ward Committee is chaired by the elected counsellor of the ward. Decisions such as park and road maintenance, provision of garbage collection, location of markets and others will be made by the Ward Committee. Furthermore, it will have the right to funds. The tenure of the Area Sabha members will be coterminous with that of the Municipality. The Community Participation Law has to make provisions for the following:

- Area Sabha within every ward
- Elections of members for each Area Sabha into the Ward Committee
- Funds, functions and functionaries for the Ward Committee

Thus, the law should create the third tier of government (or the first tier, looking bottom-up) ensuring participation of residents at the grassroots level in decision-making through the Ward Committees.

The Ward Committee is supposed be entrusted with the following functions:

1. Supervision of municipal work
2. Monitoring of water and sanitation requirements
3. Identification of slums and their up-gradation

4. Enforcing building bye-laws
5. Evaluating the Area Sabha needs
6. Public health – information dissemination
7. Environment protection
8. Area Planning
9. Data collection
10. Identification of people for subsidies

The Nagara Raj Bill is an attempt to devolve power in urban areas. It envisages creation of Area Sabhas that will elect members into the Ward Committees, which is supposed to help increasing participation of citizens in local governance.[22] The Community Participation Law also provides for public consultation in the course of preparing a city development plan to implement the reforms. GHMC in its document on the city development plan process mentions the participation of CSOs in the process of preparing the city development plan. It has also considered CSOs as one of the major stakeholders stating: "A key feature of consultations is inclusion of the representatives from poor community groups such as community development societies and self-help groups in the entire process including the working groups."[23] However, representatives of CSOs are not confident that this consultation will happen, but instead will only exist on paper.[24]

Nevertheless, so far, the Community Participation Law has hardly come into being in Andhra Pradesh. The lack of implementing decentralised democracy in urban governance so far illustrates the difficulty India has had in overcoming its centralised governmental structure and the extremely hierarchical nature of its enormous and powerful bureaucracy. Not enough, this bureaucracy has been heavily integrated into the representative side of governing as well. At all levels of India's democracy, most executive powers are paradoxically not held by elected officials, but rather by unelected bureaucrats.[25]

Many of the decisions (or lack of decisions) made in Hyderabad involving commercial and residential building rights, land tenure of the poor (e.g. Musi-River area) and waste disposal have been characteristic for the transparency problem and the lack of accountability.

---

[22] Centre for Civil Society
[23] GHMC Hyderabad – City Development Plan, Chapter – 1, 5–8
[24] Interviews with representatives of different CSOs in Hyderabad.
[25] Morris (2002)

In the case of Hyderabad, the city administration as well as numerous NGOs is interested and sometimes active in the field of political participation. The Centre for Good Governance (Hyderabad)[26], for instance, has published plenty of working materials in order to support and introduce participatory-approach solutions and intervention planning in the area of good governance. Also, HUDA's Masterplan 2010 underlines the necessity of civic engagement for the realisation of planned projects.[27] As early as 1984, HUDA found in a study on „Conservation of Historical Buildings and Areas in Hyderabad City" that „the success of urban conservation [and with that also other urban planning processes – the author] will [...] largely depend on the extent of public support received [...]". The author of this study, S. P. Shorey[28] first explains the applied methods of citizen participation (e.g. publishing newspaper articles on the issues, showing exhibitions on the topic, discussing it in school classes and presenting exemplary projects).[29]

4.1.1 Participatory Planning in Rural Kerala

While the 74th Amendment, through which urban local authorities were supposed to be created, has hardly been institutionalised in urban areas, there has been quite a progress in creating Panchayati Raj institutions, i.e. local authorities on the village level, in rural areas according to the 73rd Amendment. The state of Kerala has been progressive in endowing these newly empowered rural local government institutions with powers to plan projects on the local level with the People's Plan Campaign.

After the Panchayat and Municipality Act were passed in 1993 to strengthen Panchayati Raj and Nagarapalika institutions, the government of Kerala launched the People's Plan Campaign for Ninth Plan (5-Year-Plan) in 1996, with the aim to decentralise planning. Until then, the role of Panchayati Raj and Nagarpalika was rather limited if not restricted, principally to traditional civic functions and plans were exclusively formulated by the central and state governments in accordance with the guidelines of the Planning Commission of India. Now, the newly elected local-self-government institutions had the mandate to formulate their own local development plans with funds assigned to them (1/3 of the State Plan Fund). This was a new idea with no precedent in India. The state government issued Plan Formulation Guidelines that prescribes the participatory

---

[26] www.cgg.gov.in/cgg_home.html
[27] Cf. HUDA Masterplan 2010, p. 8
[28] Mr. S.P. Shorey is now the head of the Centre for Good Governance.
[29] INTACH (Indian Trust for Art and Cultural Heritage), for instance, acquired a great number of members with the help of newspapers which have helped to support plenty of projects all over India.

process in seven phases. As a first step, the needs of the locality had to be identified by the people in the Gramasabha (village meeting) or the Wardsabha (ward meeting). All voters in the constituency of a local body are members of the Grama or Wardsabha. The Gramasabha is held in a semi-structured way, consisting of group discussions in working groups and plenary sessions in the sectors of production, service and infrastructure. After assessing the needs of the people, each local body, in cooperation with the people, prepares a development report for each sector. The reports are discussed in the Gramasabha and copies submitted to the Planning Commission. Thereafter, interventions to meet the needs of the locality and to solve the prevailing problems were proposed and strategies for development were set, in order to prioritise the proposed interventions. This is done in a development seminar at panchayat (village council) level in the presence of experts, representatives from the Gramasabhas and other stakeholders. The District Planning Committee then has to evaluate and approve the development plan with the assistance of Technical Advisory Committees (TAC) that consist of mandatory government officials, retired officials and experts. The TAC cannot question the priority or acceptability of the plans, but only examines whether they are technically viable and economically feasible.[30]

In the context of fostering citizen participation, the Kerala participatory planning experiment forms an important step and experiment that could be transferred to urban areas. The strengths of the participatory planning process are obvious and have already been elaborated in the previous chapters. The local people are able to identify their locally specific needs; there is a greater transparency in planning resulting in reduced corruption and a greater ownership of projects by the people. A strong system of Grama Sabhas is the indispensable foundation of good governance.

But the participatory planning process has its weaknesses as well. The participation of people did not rise to the expected level and the attendance in the Gramasabhas is decreasing over the years. Especially the participation of middle and higher income classes and the educated community has to be increased. Some Elected Representatives do not take people into confidence and resort to patronage, favouritism and regionalism. Furthermore some of the constituted bodies like the TAC or the District Planning Committee do not function in the way they are supposed to. According to George (2006) the big size of the Gramasabha in Kerala with an average population of 1,500 to 2,000 and the heterogeneity of the people in a ward, have contributed to a lack of

---

[30] Lakshmanan (2006). A detailed description of participatory planning in Kerala can be found in Balan; Retna Raj (2006).

feeling of ownership of one's Gramsabha. Therefore, she sees a need for more micro level organisational forms. Their role can be seen in motivating and enabling people to participate in development planning and implementation processes and in strengthening of the Gramasabhas. Balan (2006) even states that the Gramasabhas do not function properly as democratic institutions. They are not conceived as institutions that are required to perform certain tasks or reach certain goals. Instead, they have been reduced to the level of beneficiary groups or recommendatory bodies.

From the description of some projects by Balan (2006), it also seems that the Panchayati Raj institutions have not been endowed with the respective financial means to implement the planned projects. He describes two projects, where the village people have built a bridge and introduced a micro-hydel project. In both cases substantial amounts of money and time were invested by the villagers themselves. In this case, it is questionable, whether the Panchayati Raj institutions are hardly more than civil society organisations that take care of their own affairs where government has failed.

Nevertheless, the Gramasabha can be a very good forum for social audit and for ensuring transparency and accountability. Hence, more stakeholders have to be integrated in the process to make it livelier and make it a forum for direct democracy. After all, the practice of local democracy is also a forum of political education, where people are learning to organise, to question established patterns of authority and to demand their rights. This learning enhances their preparedness for local democracy and for political participation in general.[31]

It shows that there are attempts at creating participatory planning systems by some governments, and that the local institutions can serve as more decentralised participatory planning institutions. With the introduction of the above-mentioned community participation law such planning powers could also be handed over to urban local government bodies.

Although these institutions have not yet been institutionalised in urban areas, the system and the informal creation of these bodies can still be an approach to try to influence decision-making in urban areas. This approach has recently been taken by the Tarnaka Residents' Welfare Association with the Tarnaka Experiment described in the next chapter.

---

[31] Lakshmanan (2006)

4.1.2 Hyderabad: The Tarnaka Experiment of the Tarnaka Residents' Welfare Association

Local associations in Indian cities include residents' welfare associations (RWAs) which are associations of residents of one or more houses or apartment building that are mainly concerned with issues of public services like water, electricity and street lighting, road maintenance and solid waste management – issues that concern the direct neighbourhood of the residents. There is a large numbers of RWAs in Hyderabad, but most of them are merely management committees, to which residents are legally obligated to pay charges. They in turn look after maintenance and security of the buildings and perhaps organise celebrations on major holidays.[32] However, they do not attempt to address any greater community or citywide issues. An exemption in Hyderabad is the Tarnaka Residents' Welfare Association (TRWA), which was founded with the belief that citizens participation is a part of decision-making in the community and that citizens should play an active role in the maintaining of their communities. Since 2001, the Standing Committee of Tarnaka Residents' Welfare Association (SCOTRWA) has been addressing community level issues through citizen participation. The "Tarnaka Experiment" is reputed to be a trendsetter in urban self-management with the instrumentality of the RWAs. Urban Indian society has traditionally been seen as rather indifferent towards public participation in civic and political matters and for the most part, this stereotype holds true for Hyderabad, as well. But the Tarnaka Experiment is trying to set an example in the other direction. It is a nationally as well as internationally notable community concept, which is–disappointed due to a lack of political mediation through representation at the level of urban governance–trying to find new forms of self-management and development within its small range of community level going beyond the mere management of their apartment or housing complexes.

Tarnaka is the 100th ward in East Hyderabad, with a population of nearly 80,000, of whom around 60 % are from a middle-income group with expanding incomes. About 15 to 17 % are of modest income, earning nevertheless a relatively low income of about Rs. 36,000 per year[33] per family and living in very modest housing. Another 2 to 3 % are annual immigrants, who settle on vacant places in huts. Further, there are another 20 % who own individual houses worth more than half a million Rupees (ca. 9,000 €). RWAs are commonly found in higher income or middle-class areas of cities. Youth and senior

---

[32] Harriss (2005)

[33] Statistically, those who earn less than Rs. 24,000 per year are considered as belonging to the Below Poverty Line category.

citizens comprise 15 % of the population each. Working women are about 30 to 35 % of the female population.[34]

Being actually a federation of local RWAs, the Tarnaka Residents Welfare Association represents the residents of over 200 apartment buildings in the area today. A decisive role in the success of the Tarnaka Experiment can be attributed to the leadership of Mr. Rao Chelikani, who has been constantly promoting the idea that many issues of the community can be rectified at the local level instead of calling on the government to act. The reasoning behind this is, on the hand, that people are more motivated and comfortable to handle issues they are concerned with among themselves and show more ownership for projects they have initiated themselves. On the other hand, the authorities have mostly shown to be unwilling to act on the problems of the community.

As mentioned earlier (see Chapter 4.1), despite the 74th Amendment, the legislative has so far not provided for local level decentralised democracy mechanisms (like the Gram Sabhas in rural areas) for urban areas. Therefore the TRWA holds informal annual Ward Sabhas (Ward meetings), comparable to the rural Gram Sabhas, which are organised with officials and community members to discuss pressing problems of the community. Within the Ward Sabha a micro-plan for the area is developed on the basis of a survey among the community members regarding the priority concerns of the residents. The focus of the Ward Sabha and the micro-plan is the development of solutions that cannot be solved locally rather than the presentation of problems. These are then presented to the officials for public response. Finding the distribution of Ward committees insufficient (only one corporator responsible for a ward consisting of a population of not less than 30,000), the TRWA formed an informal people's Ward committee composed of all residents welfare associations and the government corporator as the ex-officio chairperson. This Ward committee meets once a month to solve everyday problems and follow the micro-plan designed by the Ward Sabha. In reality, it has been noticed, though, that officials rarely participate in the meetings. Nevertheless, this approach is unique for Hyderabad's residents' welfare associations.[35]

Other successful activities of the TRWA are, amongst others, are the saving of a green space in Tarnaka from encroachment and turning it into a public park, getting funds and land from the city administration to build a public library, improving the community's water drainage, forming a community pact between consumers and local shop keepers to raise quality and fairness of local business practices. Some more issues are also handled

---

[34] See Megacity Pilot Project Report Number 6.
[35] SCOTRWA's pamphlet (2009)

by filing Public Interest Litigation suits, for example to save a local lake from encroachment. Other activities include awareness raising campaigns, for instance, for the Right to Information Act.

The success of the Tarnaka Experiment can be attributed to the high proportion of middle-class residents and well-educated and fairly influential residents (doctors, professors, lawyers). The economic influence has certainly played a role in accessing influential officials. Furthermore, there are many senior citizens in Tarnaka, who can spare the time and their experiences to in improving the community.

Nevertheless, the TRWA faces difficulties in motivating and activating the community members to participate, develop their own solutions and take action. Often there is resignation among the people about their inability to change anything, due also to the fact that past efforts have not shown the maximum expected results. The TRWA faces managerial problems in mobilising people, as nobody thinks it possible either to change or improve the communication techniques or to refine the tools to inform people differently.

According to Harriss (2005) RWAs are often isolated from other civil society organisations and are rarely federated together. This also holds true for Hyderabad. However, in 2008, on the initiative of SCOTRWA, more than twenty RWAs from different parts of Hyderabad formed the United Federation of Resident Welfare Associations (UFERWAS). The primary objective of UFERWAS is to bring together all independent resident welfare associations on a common platform for collective action. It is designed to help those citizens, who are frustrated by delays and broken promises of development from elected representatives, by advocating independence from 'middlemen' and taking up the developmental activities on its own. In UFERWAS members of different welfare associations have the opportunity to share with each other their experiences in their respective residential welfare associations and to discuss and develop strategies to solve problems through joint initiative (see Chapter 5.2.16).[36]

4.2 The Role of Civil Society in Mobilising and Advocating for More Transparency, Accountability and Better Public Service

While the People's Plan Campaign in Kerala, for example, was induced by the Government of Kerala to foster citizens' participation in planning, the following two chapters

---

[36] The Hindu (2008), March 2nd and The Hindu (2009), October 30th

describe two examples, where civil society first challenged the system, criticised the government and advocated for the citizens and finally became a partner of the government to make them responsive to the needs of the citizens.

4.2.1 The Role of a Civil Society Organisation in Mobilising and Advocating for the Right to Information

Notwithstanding the Constitutional provisions and Supreme Court judgements, the real movement for the right to information in India–which finally led to the enactment of the Right to Information Act in 2005–originated from a civil society organisation, the Mazdoor Kisan Shakti Sangathan (MKSS) in Rajasthan. This mass-based organisation led people to ask for copies of bills and names of persons who had received wages within projects for the construction of schools and other public infrastructure recorded in government files. On paper these infrastructure projects were all completed, but it was common knowledge, that many of the structures were missing roofs, walls and windows or were constructed with poor quality material. After years of insisting, finally the MKSS was provided with the information, which revealed that the muster rolls contained ghost entries of persons who did not exist or had died years before.

The MKSS organised the first ever People's hearing (Jan Sunwai) in Rahjasthan and invited all parties involved to defend themselves. Although, understandably, most Government officials stayed away, the news of the case spread fast all over India and led to the genesis of a broader discourse on the Right to Information in India. Also, Loksatta, then a CSO in Andhra Pradesh (Loksatta has now turned into a political party), has undertaken mass awareness campaigns on the enactment of a right to information law.

This movement, led by CSOs all over the country, could no longer be ignored and a working group was set up by the Government of India, which drafted a Bill on Freedom to Information in 1997. Notably, the draft law was criticised for not adopting a high enough standard of disclosure.

Meanwhile, MKSS's advocacy gave rise to the National Campaign on People's Right to Information (NCPRI) and the Forum for Right to Information was founded. These two organisations drafted a bill and submitted it anonymously to the Government of India. The Government of India then introduced a Freedom of Information Bill in 2000, which was passed as the Freedom of Information (FoI) Act in 2002, but was even more disappointing. It took another three years and the intervention by the Supreme Court through a PIL filed by the NCPRI, until the Right to Information Act was finally enacted in October 2005, taking into account recommendations of civil society groups.[37]

4.2.2 From Assistance to Becoming a Partner in Governance – The Citizen Report Card by the Public Affairs Centre in Bangalore

The Bangalore Citizen's Report Card, which was pioneered by the Bangalore based CSO "Public Affairs Centre", provides an assessment of the satisfaction levels of citizens with the public services in Bangalore. The first Citizen Report Card was carried out in 1994 by surveying households. The Citizen Report Card was undertaken with a view to catalyse citizens to adopt pro-active stances by demanding more accountability, accessibility and responsiveness from public service providers, to serve as a diagnostic tool for service providers, external consultants and analysts/researchers, to encourage public agencies to adopt and promote client friendly practices and policies, to design performance standards and to facilitate increased transparency in operations. The findings revealed that the level of public satisfaction with the performance of Public Service Agencies was low. A third of the urban poor surveyed had paid a bribe to public officials in the previous six months. Further, they had to make multiple visits to agencies, were ill treated by public officials, and had lower problem resolution rate (38 %) than the middle-income households (57 %).[38]

The key findings were disseminated widely to the heads of all the public agencies covered by the study and to the Chief Minister and Chief Secretary of Karnataka, to the press through a mini-seminar and to interested citizen groups and other non-governmental organisations. Many newspapers and magazines prominently displayed these findings and highlighted the issue of corruption in public services. In 1994, after the completion of the first Citizen Report Card, the country's premier daily, The Times of India, ran a feature for two months focusing on one report card finding at a time every day. Similarly a series of "openhouse" meetings were organised in the city for citizen groups who were mostly unaware of each other's existence.

In his response, the Chief Minister came forward to initiate the Bangalore Agenda Task Force, which acted as a bridge between service providers and the users. The benefits of the Citizen Report Cards project are dependent on several factors. Firstly, the media and and the publicity play an important role. Further an active civil society is needed that

---

[37] Information in this chapter from CGG (2006) and www.nyayabhoomi.org/treatise/history/history1.htm.

[38] Ravindra (2004)

continues to press for needed reforms and to monitor to which extent the reforms actually occur. Furthermore, of course, the government agencies, especially the leadership, have to show responsiveness to the findings of the Report Card. The Citizen Report Card was the first of its kind in the world, and has since then been replicated in other Indian cities such as Ahmendabad, Chennai, Delhi, Hyderabad, Mumbai and Pune. The PAC has also undertaken a similar report card assessment at the provincial and national levels through a Millennial Survey of select states across India. The Industries Department in Karnataka has adopted the Report Card approach to get feedback from industrialists to improve governance in the industry sector.[39] Dr. Samuel Paul, the initiator of the Citizen Report Card and founder of the Public Affairs Centre rates the success of the initiatives as follows:

> *We, as a small group, simply made [the report card] possible. We put it out and one of the things that happened in Bangalore, a whole plethora, a mix of new groups, forums, coalitions emerged subsequently. [...] Today, there are hundreds, literally hundreds NGOs, including the newspapers. In 1994, I couldn't find many NGOs. They were still working on purely poverty program. They were contracting things for the government. They were hesitant to speak out and express their voice on civic issues. That has changed. [...] Discussions with each of the agencies in Bangalore have taken place. [...] People are ready and willing to sit and talk about these issues. That's a kind of transformation that has taken place that can lead to partnerships. But the fact is that transformation is taking place.*[40]

4.3 Legal Means of Citizen Participation and Access to Information in India

4.3.1 Public Interest Litigation

Public Interest Litigation (PIL) is a progressive – and in most other countries uncommon – feature of the Indian system which allows organisations or individuals to take legal action on behalf of a third party. It is most often used in cases where the person or persons directly affected by an illegal action are unable (financially, emotionally, physically, due to illiteracy) to fight the case themselves. PIL is thus an important forum

---

[39] ibid.
[40] Speech by Mr. Samuel Paul, founder of PAC www.adb.org/Documents/Events/2003/Reg_Seminar_Loc_Gov_Service_Delivery_Poor/Citizens_Role_Service_Del.pdf.

for civil society to stake their claims. PIL has been on the rise since the 1980ies[41] and CSOs have increasingly used PIL to stake their claims. While most of the cases dealt with social issues until the 1980ies, their contents changed to environmental issues and those of administrative behaviour in the 1990ies. This can be attributed to the fact that PIL is increasingly initiated by elites, making this progressive legal instrument more and more dominated by the middle and upper class.[42]

Through PIL courts have been forced to assume the role of activators and regulators. And some groundbreaking decisions have been made by the courts in the sector of consumer and environmental protection.[43] However, the impact of PIL is limited due to the lack of power of enforcement of the courts and an inherently slow judicial administration.[44]

The enforcement problem has become so endemic that the Supreme Court of India was recently forced to make a statement demonstrating how desperate the situation has become: "Passing of appropriate orders requiring the implementation of the law cannot be regarded as the court having usurped the functions of the legislature or the executive."[45] Although filing and winning PILs is in itself a form of participation, its adversarial nature can weaken chances of an outside organisation being further integrated into the decision-making processes of a government. In addition to this, the territorially combative nature of India's democratic institutions illustrated here should make one realise, that if those already carrying authority and weight inside the government cannot make enforcement agencies comply with the law, the chance of those outside the government getting a foot in the door to begin participating in decision-making processes are exceedingly slim. Indeed, the lack of institutional desire to bring in other stakeholders in most instances has been both daunting and unabashedly obvious for those attempting to begin affecting change in the system, such as the massive CSO movement, which has emerged on the scene in recent decades.

Despite the successes of some PIL decisions, there are many instances where the PIL decisions are ignored. Regarding the enforcement of PIL, Dembowski states that "in the Indian context, the enforcement of judgements can no more be taken for granted than the implementation of laws. This comes as little surprise, as both would have to be

---

[41] Perhaps due to the preceding phases of emergency in 1975 and 1977, which made the members of the Indian middle-class more aware of the importance of the rule of law, perhaps due to the disrespect of the law by many officials.

[42] Dembowski (2001)

[43] Dohrmann, Fischer (2000)

[44] Dembowski (2001)

[45] Quoted from: Rama Rao, in Forum for a Better Hyderabad (2006), p. 14

carried out by the very same administrative bodies."[46] Two examples pertaining to water issues in Hyderabad, where compliance with court orders has not yet happened, are the cases of Hyderabad's two primary drinking-water sources–the lakes Himayatsagar and Osmansagar–and the case of Pattanchuru Village. In these cases, the Supreme Court of India declared that, because of the industries in the surrounding areas, the water is polluted and that the pollution has to be stopped and the people be provided with clean drinking water. However, the industries are going unpunished, as the Andhra Pradesh government has refused to enforce the court's decisions.[47]

4.3.2 The Right to Information Act

Access to information is one aspect of citizen participation. In the context of India an example of participation through information is publication of the Union and state annual budget by the central and state government. Any citizen of India can access any information about various development schemes.

For enhancing the access to information and thus the possibilities of citizens' participation in governance the enactment of the Right to Information (RTI) Act in October 2005, has been a major breakthrough. Interestingly, the introduction of the RTI Act has its roots in a CSO's mobilising and advocating for the right to information, as described in earlier (Chapter 4.2.1). The RTI Act gives citizens and CSOs the possibility to evaluate and monitor the government's actions. Civil society can thus take the role of a "watch-dog".

Getting entitlements from the government prior to the enactment of the RTI Act 2005, for example, "was a difficult task as officers often said that there was no budget allocated, there was no supply or that the stocks had finished. Now, citizens can ask for all the details of a development programme like budget, name of beneficiaries, stock etc. under the RTI Act."[48] The RTI Act opens the possibility to citizens and CSOs to monitor, review and evaluate the government's programmes and schemes. The system of RTI is widely used by CSOs to seek information from the government. "CSOs can infuse greater transparency and accountability in the administration of developmental programmes and arrest the abuse of power and misuse of public resources with the help of the RTI Act."[49]

---

[46] Dembowski (2001), p. 60
[47] Dr. Jeevananda Reddy, in Forum for a Better Hyderabad (2006), pp. 23–27 and Interview with Captain J. Rama Rao of FORUM for a better Hyderabad.
[48] PRIA (2008), p 12
[49] CGG (2006), p. 7

The Right to Information Act includes, in short, the following:

Table 1: Right to Information Act (RTI)

It includes the right to –
1. inspect works, documents, records.
2. take notes, extracts or certified copies of documents or records.
3. take certified samples of material.
4. obtain information in form of printouts, diskettes, floppies, tapes, video cassettes or in any other electronic mode or through printouts.

What is the role of Central/State Governments?
- Develop educational programmes for the public especially disadvantaged communities, on RTI.
- Encourage Public Authorities to participate in the development and organisation of such programmes.
- Promote timely dissemination of accurate information to the public.
- Train officers and develop training materials.
- Compile and disseminate a User Guide for the public in the respective official language.
- Publish names, designated postal addresses and contact details of *Public Information Officer's* (PIO) and other information such as notices regarding fees to be paid, remedies available in law if request is rejected etc.

Who are (PIOs)?
PIOs are officers designated by the public authorities in all administrative units or offices under them to provide information to the citizens requesting information under the Act. Any officer whose assistance has been sought by the PIO for the proper discharge of his or her duties, shall render all assistance and, for the purpose of contraventions of the provisions of this Act, such other officer shall be treated as a PIO.

Source: Adapted from: http://righttoinformation.gov.in

However, the RTI Act has not been fully implemented in all the states. Some states have taken initiatives to facilitate easier access to information, while in a large number of states citizens are still not provided information on time. The overall implementation of RTI in the country has been rather slow. According to a study by the Society for Participatory Research in Asia the RTI Act is not yet functioning as mandated by the Act at all. Besides it being hard for citizens to allocate the Public Information Officers (PIOs) responsible within the administration due to missing directories, many requests for information are not answered in the mandated time frame and a significant amount of appeals is not answered at all. Many citizens who have sought for information had to visit the public authority several times until they were provided with the requested information. Further, there are complaints that the PIOs do not cooperate in providing information to citizens and cases even of harassment and threats by the PIOs are abundant. A representative of the Confederation of Voluntary Associations (COVA), Hyderabad, also expressed their disappointment about getting information through the RTI Act. COVA has filed more than a hundred applications for information, but only very few of them have been answered. Thus, although the RTI Act could be a powerful tool of citizen participation, if implemented in the manner mandated, its current implementation falls short of its actual scope.

4.4 Constraints for Public Participation

One of the primary difficulties facing the masses (lower classes) in participating meaningfully in governing processes in developing societies with open corruption such as India is the fact that a significant portion of the population has other things, namely basic livelihood necessities, to worry about and that therefore issues such as corruption or transparency or accountability take on lesser importance. Combined with the ingrained nature of corruption in the system today, poverty is therefore seen to be a major roadblock in the quest to reduce or end corruption in India and to strengthen participative processes.

The inexplicably persistent urban water problems in Hyderabad, despite the urgency to solve them and their obvious nature, demonstrate the problem of corruption in India. "As a result of the politicisation of the administrative machinery, the law-enforcing agencies have [become] mixed up with the very elements whose unlawful activities they are expected to check and control." This problem is fed by patronage and protection that corrupt law enforcement agencies receive from politicians, completing a "frightening triangular nexus [which] has evolved between criminals, government functionaries and politicians."[50] The "triangular nexus" is something, which has been quite apparent in Hyderabad's case of building and land rights issues.

Furthermore, the absence of pro-active information, communication and cooperation from the governments–local, state and central–poses another constraint to participation. There is a big gap between procedures and standards "on paper" and their implementation in reality. Often, actions are only taken, when they are solicited, implored or induced with some incentive. It has also been shown that it is very difficult for CSOs

---

[50] Jain, R.B. and Bawa, P.S. (2004), p. 35

in Hyderabad to get attention from the local authorities for their causes, and often their attempts at seeking involvement in decision-making has been in vain (e.g. in the Metro Rail Project). The willingness of local authorities to cooperate with civil society organisations has been described as rather low.

Another, yet quite similar, problem are the unclear responsibilities of the different public authorities who often assume no responsibility for a certain matter and instead assign the responsibility to another public authority causing the requester to move from authority to authority, which is often interpreted as a lack of willingness of the public authorities to cooperate. These factors are also main causes of political distrust.

Not surprisingly, also in India participatory processes are being abused by groups that labour against democracy. In her book "Partizipation und die Politik der Gewalt: Hindunationalismus und Demokratie in Indien" Julia Eckert describes the structure of action of Shiv Sena ('Army of Shiva'), a nationalist political party, which is active primarily in Maharashtra, especially in and around Mumbai. Particularly deprived people are taking part in the programmes of Shiv Sena, which promise "community", "deliverance" and participation in the political power. Shiv Sena is organised through neighbourhood- and local associations, which offer social services, like ambulance, water supply or infrastructure improvements. The book explains methods of the party such as antagonism as part of their program and violence as ideology and method.[51] It shows limitations and difficulties of participation and its methods within a society of people with various financial and cultural backgrounds. Such developments make the further development and adaptation of participatory methods and tools to local contexts even more important. Particularly in the areas of social equality, economic efficiency, ecological balance and political stability developing a societal consensus, including all related population groups, is a crucial goal of participation. Participation is not only a method or a tool, it must be understood as a civil task.[52]

Following these examples, participatory processes are theoretically established but still not easily realised due to political conditions and especially not sufficiently used: "[...] further progress of democratic practice in India must crucially depend on enriching the participatory processes. [...] Much will depend on the possibility of enhancing public participation more widely."[53]

---

[51] Eckert (2004)
[52] Jentsch (2002)
[53] Drèze, Jean/ Sen, Amartya (2002), p. 379

5 Stakeholder Analysis with Focus on the Civil Society Sector

5.1 Purpose and Methodology of the Analysis

Development processes don't evolve in a linear way, but are a permanent negotiation of interests, opinions and ideas between all persons and institutions involved in the process: the stakeholders. The first step of any participatory process is the identification of stakeholders. Who are the people, groups and organisations who have significant and legitimate interests in specific urban issues? Stakeholders are those whose interests are affected, who possess information, resources and expertise needed for strategy formulation and implementation, and who control relevant implementation instruments. A stakeholder analysis explores the relevance of each stakeholder involved in a topic or sector, its goals and interests, its strengths and flaccidities and its relation to others. It is a useful tool in participatory urban governance for identifying people, groups, institutions and organisations having significant and legitimate interests in specific issues. However, the analysis by itself only identifies potentially relevant stakeholders – it does not ensure that they will become active partners in the project. Nevertheless, as indicated in the stakeholder map, some of the CSOs are already active partners of the Sustainable Hyderabad project (TRWA, Forum for a better Hyderabad, Goethe-Center).

Needless to say, though, that the city government or the metropolitan planning authority is going to play a central role in dealing with potential problems of participatory planning. The government has to transfer substantial powers to the citizens enabling them to take decisions, and it has to guarantee that the decisions made through the participatory process are indeed implemented. Government thus has the role of an initiator, enabler and facilitator and has to acknowledge and support the participatory process as an outside agent. It has to be especially active in getting the process started, it should not have a leading role within the participatory arena and it has to leave the contents and the steering of the process mainly to the participants. Thus, government's role has a dual function: as constructor of an enabling environment for community participation and civic engagement, on the one hand, and as a controlling force, ensuring that the administration is credible and willing to work with the population, on the other. With sustainability as a main target in the decision-making process, keeping environmental issues in mind may be seen as a third task. Furthermore, the scientific and economic sectors play a crucial role in the exchange of information, knowledge and concepts and in implementation.

The CSOs were identified through recommendations of existing partners in Hyderabad, through internet research and recommendations by the organisations already interviewed. In addition, we have mainly identified CSOs whose activities are linked to the set of problems of the project: "Energy Efficiency and Climate Change". Furthermore, we have included several important CBOs or groups of CBOs in Hyderabad, such as Residents Welfare Organisations, in the study, which mainly address the immediate problems of their community, and thus mostly have no *specific* engagement in the above topics, but have broad member bases of affected citizens.

To gather information on civil society organisations, interviews with representatives of the organisations were conducted. In addition, on- and offline research via the organisations' website, their newsletters and publications was done. Needless to say, that this compilation is not complete, but rather shows a small fraction of CSOs in Hyderabad.

The following topics were covered in the interviews:

- Mission and aims
- Focus of activities
- Main activities in the last two years, e.g. events and implemented projects, and their outcomes
- Achievements / Success of activities
- Role/Function for the people/within society
- Special knowledge / strengths / capacities
- Possible weaknesses/difficulties
- Cooperation with/relation to other NGOs, policy-makers and economy

5.2 Stakeholder Mapping

The stakeholder map below (Figure 1) shows the stakeholders in the civil society sector on the national, state and local (Hyderabad) level (shown in the grey framed rectangles), and also takes into account the role of the business and scientific sector and public authorities.

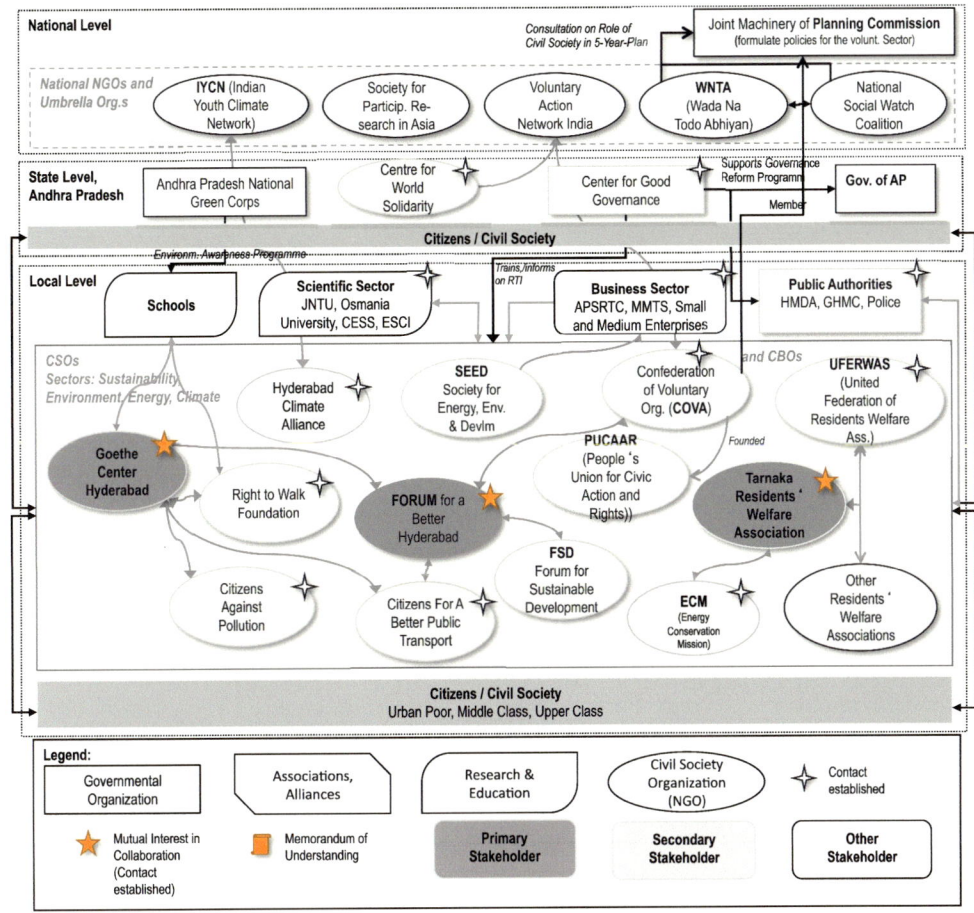

Figure 1: Stakeholder Map
Source: own illustration

The civil society organisations are shown in the grey coloured rectangles. At the national level these are mainly umbrella organisations, which represent local or regional (or also national) civil society organisations at the national level. At the local level the focus is on civil society organisations (on the left side) that are engaged in the topics of sustainability, energy, environment and climate and community based organisations (right side), in this case the residents' welfare organisations. These play a crucial role for the project, as they directly represent different communities of Hyderabad and thus have a broad member base. In addition, they mainly represent the urban middle class, which is an important target group of the project, as the emerging middle class is increasingly obtaining the financial opportunities for more energy-consuming lifestyles.

Furthermore, the scientific and economic sectors play a crucial role as stakeholders for the exchange of information, knowledge and concepts and in the implementation. Of course, the public authorities are important stakeholders for cooperation, as they have to devolve substantial powers to the citizens and implement or take into account the decisions made by civil society.

The black arrows represent a rather institutionalised cooperation, while the grey arrows represent informal cooperation or networks. As can be noted from the stakeholder map, some of the CSOs in Hyderabad cooperate with each other while others, for example the residents' welfare associations are rather isolated – with maybe the exemption of the Tarnaka Residents' Welfare Association. The Hyderabad Climate Alliance, for example, is rather a spin off of the national Indian Youth Climate Network and does not seem to be very much linked to many local CSOs.

The following table gives an overview of the main fields of action of the analysed stakeholders that already play an important role within the project or could be of importance as stakeholders, partners or multipliers for the project.

Table 3: List of stakeholders

No.	Stakeholder	Key Interests/Fields of Action
	Governmental Stakeholders	
1	Centre for Good Governance (CGG)	Coordinates and supports the design and implementation of GoAP's Governance Reform Programme. It undertakes action research, provides professional advice to, and conducts change management programmes for government departments and agencies to help them implement their reform agenda successfully.
2	Andhra Pradesh National Green Corps (APNGC)	Raising awareness through activities; Teacher's training; Preparing study material for schools; Coordination
3	GHMC Greater Hyderabad Municipal Corporation	
4	HMDA Hyderabad Municipal Development Authority	

Table 3: List of stakeholders (continued)

No.	Stakeholder	Key Interests/Fields of Action
5	**Business Sector**	e.g. APSRTC, MMTS, Small and Medium Entreprises
6	**Scientific Sector**	Osmania University, JNTU, CESS
	Civil Society Organisations	
7	Society for Participatory Research in Asia (PRIA)	Works at several national as well as international levels to promote governance, people's participation, development and empowerment by participatory research and strengthening knowledge.
8	Indian Youth Climate Network (IYCN)	Generates awareness about climate change, in India and internationally, distributes actual information on the topic and events related to the topic.
9	Centre for World Solidarity (CWS)	Voluntary Organisation aiming at creating a more equitable Indian society through issue and environment based programmes. Working through a network of stakeholders and individuals to promote participatory development.
10	Association of German Culture, Hyderabad - Goethe Zentrum	The primary aim of Goethe-Centre is to promote knowledge of the German language, German culture and foster intercultural cooperation.
11	Hyderabad Climate Alliance	Coalition of individuals and organisations interested in and committed to the cause of environmental awareness raising. It is a youth movement to bring together local efforts of individuals, organisations and institutions with the aim of mitigating climate change and helping the people of Hyderabad and Andhra Pradesh adapt to its impacts.
12	Right to Walk Foundation (R2W)	Creates awareness among the people on their rights as pedestrians, educate the Government and the Citizens of Hyderabad about the importance of footpaths and save their disappearance and misuse.
13	Citizens against pollution (CAP)	Launching programmes aimed at bringing water, air, noise pollution into public/political notice; Networking with other institutions, cooperating with other initiatives (e.g. to carry out studies to probe real pollution)

Table 3: List of stakeholders (continued)

No.	Stakeholder	Key Interests/Fields of Action
14	Citizens for Better Public Transport in Hyderabad (CBPTH)	Generating a public debate and involve the civil society on the options for public transportation in Hyderabad (no elevated metro system but Improvement of the already existing MMTS); Implementation of measures to reduce congestion
15	Forum for a Better Hyderabad (FORUM)	The only environmental organisation to be accepted by the authorities of Hyderabad as a partner in governance. Acting constructively and proactively, to mobilise public opinion, and to speak loudly in a unified voice where transparency is lacking or where there is a lack of adequate consideration of environmental issues by decision makers.
16	Society for Energy, Environment and Development (SEED)	Create awareness about the Environment and Energy issues. It also aims at creating devices to enhance the quality of life. It promotes community development activities under a fourfold programme of employment, self-help, health and education.
17	Forum for Sustainable Development (FSD)	Create public awareness, to build informed public support, and pressure through democratic means; Topics: GM crops/ issues of corporatisation of agriculture, protection of lake bodies in Hyderabad, more transparency and public debate with regard to Metro Rail project in Hyderabad
18	Society for Preservation of Environment and Quality of Life (SPEQL)	Awareness raising in the area of water, waste, conservation of energy and water; Organisation of movement for control of air, noise pollution and particularly in urban areas; Awareness-raising in observing traffic rules and discipline; Efficient mass transport system in urban areas; Promotion of urban forestry
19	Energy Conservation Mission (ECM)	Promotes energy conservation awareness of the society through functional groups for various sectors- Domestic, Industry, Agricultural, Commercial, Transportation, Educational Institutions, Renewable Sources of Energy, Standards & Labelling etc.

Table 3: List of stakeholders (continued)

No.	Stakeholder	Key Interests/Fields of Action
20	Confederation of Voluntary Organisations (COVA)	A national network of over 800 organisations working for the vision of communal harmony, peace and social justice. Spreads awareness among the poor and marginalised sections of society about their right to basic services and to participate in the democratic process (bottom-up approach). Conducts Voter Awareness Programmes, Open Forums before the general elections.
21	People's Union for Civic Action and Rights (PUCAAR)	Evolves models that enable marginalised communities to adopt rights-based-approach to claim basic services and amenities as a matter of basic citizenship rights. Setting up Basti Committees and organise training programmes, awareness programmes on con-sumer rights, human rights and right to information.
22	United Federation for Residents' Welfare Associations (UFERWAS)	Bringing together all independent resident welfare associations on a common platform for collective action. Members of different welfare associations have the opportunity to share with each other their experiences in their respective residential welfare associations and to discuss and develop strategies to solve problems through joint initiative.
23	Tarnaka Residents Welfare Association (TRWA)	Trying to find new forms of self-management and development within its small range of community level. An informal Ward Sabha is regularly held adopts a micro-plan for the area's development.

5.2.1 The Centre for Good Governance (CGG)

The Centre for Good Governance was established by the Government of Andhra Pradesh (GoAP) in October 2001 to help it achieve the State's goal of transforming governance. CGG coordinates and supports the design and implementation of GoAP's Governance Reform Programme. It undertakes action research, provides professional advice to, and conducts change management programmes for government departments and agencies to help them implement their reform agenda successfully. It works closely with policy-makers like Ministers, senior officials, management experts, institutions and other stakeholders, especially citizens and CSOs, towards ushering a caring government, centred on the people.

Its Objectives are:

- To work with government departments and other stakeholders to analyse key issues in governance, identify solutions, help develop action plans, and support implementation of these plans and the reform agenda.
- To act as a think tank and help translate government goals, objectives and policy priorities and reform agenda into tangible reform actions with focus on principles and practices of good governance.
- To identify those areas for change that will make the most impact in improving performance and policy-making in government and enable it to respond better to the needs of the people.
- To create a bank of best practices, methodologies and tools in governance reforms including successful e-governance applications.
- To support change management and management development programmes in government to effectively carry forward governance reforms and to develop a reform communication strategy for wider implementation.
- To provide technical support and advisory services to state and local governments, national and international organisations in the areas of action research, change management, design and implementation of governance reforms, including administrative reforms.

The focus areas of the Centre for Good Governance under its current plan of activities include amongst others: simplifying government, accountable government, responsive and citizen-focused services and e-governance.

The Centre for Good Governance has published plenty of working materials in order to support and introduce participatory-approach solutions and intervention planning in the area of good governance. Furthermore, it informs and trains CSOs on how to file for information under the Right to Information Act.[54]

---

[54] Information taken from organisation's website: www.cgg.gov.in/ourvision.jsp.

5.2.2 Andhra Pradesh National Green Corps Society (APNGC)

One stakeholder playing an important role in spreading environmental awareness is the Andhra Pradesh National Green Corps Society (APNGC). APNGC is part of the National Green Corps formed by the Government of India. It comes under direct government supervision and is funded by the government. Its Chairman is the Principal Secretary of the Environment, Forests, Science and Technology Department. It performs a number of tasks like creating awareness through rallies, campaigns, conducting workshops, seminars etc; training teachers; preparing study material for schools; evaluating their environmental activities; co-coordinating activities between schools and many more.

It has its presence in 5,750 schools in Andhra Pradesh and 250 schools in Hyderabad and gives an annual grant of Rs. 2,500 each. Government schools, Indian Certificate of Secondary Education syllabus schools, Central Board of Secondary Education syllabus schools, Navodaya Schools, Tribal and Social Welfare Schools under Greater Hyderabad are all part of APNGC.

The NGC leadership has a two-tiered structure: the State Level Committee is the directorate of NGC, and the District Level Committee forms the District NGC Unit. At the district level, similar societies are formed under the concerned District Collectors. All of the District NGC committee members are represented in the District NGC Society. This committee provides resources and contacts for the school teachers who are in charge of the NGC units for undertaking activities at the school level. The school level NGC unit forms a committee with the headmaster/ headmistress of the school as the chairman and with teachers as members, who are called Green Teachers.

The main functions of the Directorate are the production of training manuals, audio-visual aids, networking, conducting state and regional level NGC events, participating in national level NGC programmes, publication of NGC newsletter, documentation and dissemination of NGC success stories, training and re-training including refresher training.

The following simple programmes are undertaken by schools initially:

- Plantation Programme
- Vermi Composting
- Rainwater Harvesting
- Cleanliness in Public Places

Apart from this, schools have awareness raising and teaching programmes, which are undertaken throughout the year depending on the season. During sewing season children are taught about the opportunity to replace chemical pesticides and fertilisers by organic pesticides and fertilisers. In June/July the attention is drawn towards plastic solid waste when the solid waste is likely to reach water bodies and likely to destroy the water quality. In July/August, when water is available in plenty, the topic of Water Conservation is addressed. In August/September, the protection of water bodies becomes an issue when there are thousands of floating idols of Lord Ganesh to be seen in all water bodies across the city. (At the end of Ganesh Chaturthi festival, all the idols are immersed in water bodies.) In September/October when people tend to use more power for heating purposes topics dealing with energy conservation are raised. When noise is produced during the Durga Puja and Diwali festivals in October/November students are taught about noise pollution and in the course of the Holi festival even the chemical colour subject is given attention.

Every school forms five natural resources management team. Students of class VIII form the Eco Club in the school and every Eco Club has a minimum of 40 students each. The students are divided into five teams and each team is headed by a leader. All students in the schools fall into either of these teams. Students can decide every year in which team they want to be active. The five teams are:

- Biodiversity management team: Responsible for flora and fauna in the school.
- Water management team: Responsible for drinking and waste water.
- Beautification team: In charge of reducing, reusing and recycling of water.
- Energy Management team: In charge of energy audit and conservation.
- Land Use Management team: Planning and conducting movement in the school

To effectively guide the students in their activities, a two-tier training programme is conducted. First, the master trainers (one or two from each district) are trained, who in turn, train the teacher's in-charge of Eco Clubs in each district. The master trainers are trained by the faculty members of State Council of Education, Research & Training (SCERT). Every year there are refresher programmes and interaction meetings for these Green Teachers to address the most typical environmental issues.

All the activities of NGC are designed to arouse curiosity and develop questioning spirit along with the ability to respond by exhibiting behavioural change in students towards their immediate environment.

The work undertaken by APNGC is well appreciated by the schools and the students. Students and parents have reportedly expressed pleasure regarding the various activities undertaken. Uniquely, APNGC is also targeting schools, which have students from middle and lower middle class backgrounds as well as tribal students. One of the aspects stressed by all the people consulted is that usually teachers who teach Science in school take up the role of Green Teacher. Instead of teachers from only one department taking up the activities all the teachers from the school should be integrated into the programme. APNGC's area of operation is vast within the city of Hyderabad and its network spans throughout the state. Due to government backing most of the schools readily take up the programmes.[55]

5.2.3 Society for Participatory Research in Asia (PRIA)

The Delhi-based non-profit organisation PRIA was formed in 1982. It is a civil society organisation working at several national as well as international levels to promote governance, people's participation, development and empowerment by participatory research and strengthening knowledge. PRIA provides training in participatory research, grassroots action and evaluation, and publishes books, manuals, worksheets and study reports on different socio-political topics concerning India for academic and government institutions and voluntary organisations.

PRIA works with marginalised groups, like women, and other socially and economically marginalised sections of society. It works for the strengthening of local government institutions and civil society. PRIA works directly in 17 states of India and extends its reach through its more than 3,000 civil society partners. Strategic partnerships with academia, media, government and international actors are important aspects of PRIA's work nationally and globally. PRIA's vision is to develop a democratic society based on the values of equity and justice. Its mission is to work towards the promotion of policies, institutions and capacities that strengthen voices and participation against the marginalisation of communities.[56]

---

[55] Information gathered from organisation's website: http://203.199.178.89/apngc/index.htmas as well as books, study material, pamphlets prepared by APNGC and discussion with project officers and Ms. Shashikala, Green Teacher.

[56] Information gathered by www.pria.org.

5.2.4 Indian Youth Climate Network

The Indian Youth Climate Network (IYCN), founded in March 2008, is a coalition of Indian youth and youth oriented organisations who are concerned about climate change. Within its short term of existence, the network has seen massive growth and has generated a lot of awareness in India and internationally. Its blog *What's With the Climate? – Voices of a Subcontinent Grappling with Climate Change* serves as an international platform and open forum that also distributes actual information on the topic and events related to the topic.

People can get involved by contributing to the projects such as Green your Workplace, your School or Campus, Campus Climate Challenge, Search for Solutions or participating in the national Rava-Tour[57] to spread national environmental awareness.

In 2008 Hyderabad celebrated a momentous occasion, as the nation's first Youth Summit on Climate Change took place, organised by the IYCN. Young people from all over India showed that they have a strong vested interest in helping to bring climate change under control because they will otherwise have to live with its increasingly severe consequences over the coming decades. The IYCN in Hyderabad is again organising the Hyderabad Youth Summit on Climate Change on June $21^{st}/22^{nd}$ 2009. A Hyderabad Youth Charter on Climate Change that shall reflect the efforts of the Indian youth concerning development and sustainability with regard to climate change is planned. Furthermore, a discourse on the implementation of practices and ideas concerning mitigation strategies across Hyderabad as well as a network of youth and government bodies is going to be established.[58]

5.2.5 Centre for World Solidarity (CWS)

Centre for World Solidarity (CWS) has been actively involved in development work in India since 1960s. It is a voluntary organisation founded as a Public Trust in 1992 to create a more equitable society. CWS works through a network of different stakeholders and individuals to promote participatory development in five states of India namely Andhra Pradesh, Tamil Nadu, Orissa, Jharkhand and Bihar. To achieve its vision of a society well aware of its rights and duties, CWS is working closely linked with grassroots civil society.

---

[57] Rava is India's first electric vehicle which was launched on May 11, 2001. The IYCN toured all over India with the Rava in spring 2009, going also through Hyderabad.

[58] Information gathered from initiatives website: www.iycn.in/about.htm.

Its key fields of action can be divided into issue based and land and environment based programmes. The issue-based programmes are projects concerning Gender, Adivasi-, Dalit -, Minority, Human as well as Child Rights, the National Dalit Forum, Panchayat Raj Initiatives and spreading HIV and Aids awareness. Environment based programmes are Centre for Sustainable Agriculture, Work on Forestry, Watershed Management, Flood Control, Environment and Social Regulators.[59]

5.2.6 Association of German Culture Hyderabad (AGCH) – Goethe Zentrum Hyderabad

The Goethe-Zentrum Hyderabad has the same primary aim as the Goethe-Institutes all over the world, which in India are called Max-Müller-Bhavans (MMB). The primary aim of Goethe-Centre therefore is to promote knowledge of the German language, German culture and foster inter-cultural cooperation.

The MMB, which existed previously in Hyderabad, was closed in 1993. After a gap of more than 10 years, the idea of opening a German centre in Hyderabad was born. The establishment of the Goethe-Centre in Hyderabad was initiated by the Goethe-Institute in New Delhi, the General Consulate of the Federal Republic of Germany in Chennai and especially through the efforts of its present Executive Director Mrs. Amita Desai. Unlike the Goethe-Institutes, the Goethe-Centre is not fully funded by the Auswärtiges Amt (German Foreign Office), but only to a certain extent and the rest to maintain the centre, is derived from the profits earned through conducting German language classes. The fact that the profits do not go back to the German Foreign Office, unlike in the case of Goethe-Institutes, helps the Goethe-Centre to sustain itself financially.

The Goethe-Centre was opened in December 2004 as the first ever Goethe-Centre in India. It is locally registered under the Andra Pradesh Societies Act. It has a local Governing Board, which consists of scientists, professionals and German experts from Hyderabad. It is also governed by the German Foreign Office and the German Embassy in Delhi is responsible for the quality and cash audits.

Besides constantly organising various cultural events with Indian, German and international artists, it is engaged in many social and developmental activities. In 2008, the Goethe-Centre organised an exhibition on the impacts of the planned Metro Rail project on Hyderbad city. In close co-operation with CSOs in Hyderabad like Right to Walk Foundation, Forum for a Better Hyderabad, Citizens for Better Public Transport Hyderabad (CBPTH) etc., it organises social events by involving school children and

---

[59] All information based on the organisation's website: www.cwsy.org and Annual Report 07/08.

citizens of Hyderabad. On 17th February, 2009, in co-operation with Right to Walk Foundation, it organised a Study-Walk with the students of Vidyaranya School to raise their awareness about the traffic situation and their rights in traffic. In the same month, Goethe-Centre and nexus institute along with PTV, Germany organised the workshop "Hyderabad Citizens' Charter for Urban Transport".[60] Through its many contacts in Hyderabad's civil society, public authorities, experts and economy the Goethe-Centre can play an important role as a multiplier.

5.2.7 Hyderabad Climate Alliance

The Hyderabad Climate Alliance is a wing of the Indian Youth Climate Network (IYCN). It was established in 2008 in the context of the Indian Youth Summit on Climate Change, the nation's first youth summit on climate change, organised by the Indian Youth Climate Network and its partners. The Hyderabad Climate Alliance is a coalition of individuals and organisations interested in and committed to the cause of environmental awareness rising. It is a youth movement to bring together local efforts of individuals, organisations and institutions with the aim of mitigating climate change and helping the people of Hyderabad and Andhra Pradesh adapt to its impacts. The launch included all 50 delegates from Hyderabad and AP signing on to the Hyderabad Climate Alliance Pledge, agreeing that they "understand that climate change is an impending global catastrophe [...] and believe that Hyderabad and Andhra Pradesh will be particularly susceptible [...] and commit [themselves] to contribute in earnest to mitigating climate change and helping the people and natural environment of Hyderabad to adapt."[61]

One of its founding members is Vikram Aditya, who also works for the World Wildlife Fund as a project consultant at the Andhra Pradesh state office. The Alliance was formed by a group of young active residents of Hyderabad who share mutual goals, and believe that articulating efforts and working collectively helps to increase the effectiveness and productivity of environmental alliances. The Hyderabad Climate Alliance wants to emphasise the effects of climate change and the severity of its impacts on India in general and the Hyderabad Deccan region in particular. It endorses drastic emission reduction through the speedy implementation of all available mitigation technologies. It gathers all partners in this field and plans different activities to raise the public awareness on

---

[60] Information compiled from www.goethe.de/hyderabad, January edition of Simply South – a magazine from India Today and Programme Brochure January 2009 of Goethe-Centre.
[61] www.globalcitizens.org.in/node/32

climate change. Present members of the Alliance include students, activists, young leaders, CSO representatives, scholars and scientists, and academics.[62]

Activities/ Projects

Hyderabad Unplug project initiated by the Hyderabad Climate Alliance is an initiative that urged people to switch off non-essential items when not in use on May 3rd 2008. During that hour, participants have also been asked to replace older light bulbs with energy efficient compact fluorescent lamps, while corporate partners have been asked to identify lasting ways to reduce energy usage.[63]

The initiative is aimed at making people more aware of their environment and at highlighting the seriousness of global warming. It is supposed to present mitigation measures and generate passion and commitment desperately needed to succeed in the effort of saving the environment. A new project is the "Paint the City Green" initiative. Hyderabad Unplug approached private and public schools and is expecting a holistic participation and commitment from various schools in making Hyderabad Green together with school children. 50,000 saplings are supposed to be distributed to children of various schools. The Children, under the guidance and support from respective school management and parents, shall be trained to plant one sapling in their respective homes or surroundings and adopt the tree for three years.

Each school will also be recommended to adopt trees at its premises and on the lane that leads to the school. Children from higher classes are recommended to be in charge of them. From each school, a moderator will be identified as a single point of contact for co-ordinating and networking the process of plantation and adoption. Each child is expected to take a photograph of the sapling on day one after a year of plantation. School managements shall follow up and maintain the drive in children through regular green activities.[64]

5.2.8 Right to Walk Foundation

In Hyderabad today, footpaths are disappearing very fast. Most of the existing ones are being used as public toilets. Safe pedestrian crossings do not exist. Footpaths in cleaner areas are being encroached by malls and retail shop owners, who use them as parking space for their customers. Road widening is being done by Greater Hyderabad Municipal Corporation (GHMC) by simply removing footpaths. Ms. Kanthimathi Kannan started

---

[62] Information gathered from IYCN's website: http://iycn.in/member_groups/ unless otherwise noted.
[63] The Hindu, April 9th, 2008
[64] www.hyderabadunplug.org

the Right to Walk Foundation (R2W) in 2005 to fight against all these maladies and make Hyderabad a pedestrian friendly city. The mission of R2W is to educate the Government and the citizens of Hyderabad about the importance of footpaths. To achieve these goals, Ms. Kannan has been submitting applications and filing petitions under the Right to Information Act (RTI Act), to urge the GHMC to make the roads pedestrian-friendly with proper footpaths.

In an RTI application dated December 10, 2007, Ms. Kannan requested the GHMC to provide her with the road plan showing pavement widths for the road from Karol Bagh colony to Sarojini Devi Eye Hospital via Nanalnagar crossroads. In March 2008 she received a reply from GHMC, in which it just informed that the responsibility of maintaining footpaths on the said road lies with the Roads and Buildings Department.

On February 1, 2008, Ms. Kannan filed an RTI application regarding permissions given by GHMC to various corporate business retail outlets. The application specifically sought for details regarding parking facilities provided by the above-mentioned outlets to their customers. Failing a response, she approached the Appellate Body in GHMC on March 17, 2008. The Additional Commissioner (Administration), GHMC in his letter stated that the Appellate Authority for this issue within GHMC was the Zonal Commissioner (Central). In a telephonic conversation on April 11, 2008, the latter directed her to Chief City Planner in the GHMC. The Chief City Planner agreed to answer her query immediately. However, that did not happen.

To create awareness among the people on their rights as pedestrians, R2W launched a '20k Signature Campaign' on October 24th 2008. Signatures of those who are most affected due to lack of footpaths like children, women, senior citizens and disabled were collected.[65] After collecting around 10,000 signatures R2W halted the process for the past one month due to elections. Ms. Kannan felt that due to elections people do not have enough time to go through the issues, which have led to the signature campaign. It will resume soon after the new government comes to power.

Apart from this, a Walkathon was conducted on Feb 17, 2009. The Goethe-Zentrum and the R2W coordinated with Vidyaranya School and conducted a 'Study Walk'. R2W also aims at conducting Walkability Studies. This is a fairly scientific method that gives a few guidelines to enable the walker to decide how walk able a stretch is. The R2W is involving students from the urban planning department of JNA and FAU, Masab Tank in the study.[66]

---

[65] The Hindu, October 25th, 2008
[66] http://therighttowalk-kanthimathi.blogspot.com

Ms. Kannan is a member of the Forum for Better Hyderabad. She is also in constant touch with other NGOs like the Confederation of Voluntary Associations (COVA), the Forum for Sustainable Development, Apna Watan and Concerned Citizens.

R2W also demands that an elected mayor be appointed for Hyderabad city with executive powers. There is a provision for appointment of an elected mayor in the rules of the Municipal Corporation. The mayor will be an elected representative and be in-charge of all aspects of city development. She thinks that the citizens will then have the possibility of contacting a single authority for the redress of their grievances. This will reduce the endless number of bureaucrats they have to meet to solve even a small problem.[67]

R2W has made good use of Right to Information Act to save footpaths. Some of its efforts have been successful. As a result, some footpaths have been restored and parking has been forbidden on them. Still a lot more needs to be done. The provisions under the Hyderabad Municipal Corporations Act, 1955 that deal with footpaths define public streets as including pavements. Section 373 entrusts such public streets to GHMC and Section 374 makes it a duty of the Commissioner to take measures for the safety of pedestrians. However, this legal framework is applicable only to roads that belong to GHMC. The legal responsibility for footpaths on highways within the city is not yet clear. As such, the GHMC and the Roads and Buildings Department are throwing the responsibility on each another for the same.[68] [69]

5.2.9 Citizens Against Pollution

Another important stakeholder is the environmental action group Citizens Against Pollution. Dr. K Purusotham Reddy is the founder president of Citizens Against Pollution, established in 1985. Citizens Against Pollution (CAP) has its' origin more or less in Dr. Reddy's brother's rose garden. After more than 10,000 rosebushes died in the family-run nursery, the brothers had the well water tested and found it polluted by a new chemical factory in the area. With the help of a local Institute of Preventive Medicine, scientific studies were carried out in the neighbourhood, and the newly founded CAP marched on government offices and the courts. CAP won victories over a starch company that was polluting the water near Osmania University's residence halls and in forcing the Nuclear Fuel Complex, a Government-run uranium enriching plant, to wall itself off from nearby

---

[67] March 19, 2009, The Times of India
[68] May 18, 2008, The Times of India
[69] All Information gathered in consultation with Ms. Kannan, founder Right to Walk foundation; as well as articles in newspapers, blogs and official website of the foundation (as directed by the founder).

residents after several children were burned with radioactive waste. Dr. Reddy was also associated with a 1990 "Citizens' Report" on pollution in Andhra Pradesh, which suggested a link between local development policies and "an international network of capitalists, capitalist governments, military power and bureaucratic steel frame."[70]

Dr. Reddy believes that real estate 'sharks'as well as people in poorer districts have erected buildings in dozens of water tank beds and canals in the city after filling them over in the last 15 years. Successive governments have turned a blind eye or actually abetted these encroachments. Today there are only 170 water bodies in and around the city from the 500, which existed 60 years ago. CAP, in a statement, said that the provincial government had also reduced by nearly 40 percent the total area of the Hussain Sagar reservoir by reclaiming land for building roads and parks. Hyderabad has dozens of small water tanks and lakes that feed water via canals into the 445-year-old Hussain Sagar reservoir in the city centre. CAP has also filed writ petition in Andhra Pradesh High Court seeking direction to save 170 lakes in Hyderabad Urban Area.[71]

CAP also brought to the fore the increasing air pollution levels in the Pasha Mailaram Industrial Estate and from 1986 onwards has been also working on the issue of industrial pollution in Patancheru. It has educated and motivated farmers to protect their lands from toxic pollution. The Supreme Court of India has extended an interim compensation to the farmers affected in this area.[72]

The strength of CAP as seen by Mr Reddy is the belief in Gandhian Principles. His methods like staging dharnas, relay hunger strikes, march to Assembly etc. are usually based on these principles. Furthermore, whenever CAP takes up an issue, Dr. Reddy advises the affected people to form a Struggle Committee. People from the affected areas become part of the committee whose membership is voluntary. The struggle committee will have a convener who will keep others abreast about developments. The committee works only for solving the issue at hand. A Struggle Committee against Nuclear Plant at Nagarjuna Sagar Dam in 1987-88 came into existence to stop the installation of a nuclear plant. People from 4 districts were mobilised for a massive public protest. This is the only success story of its kind in India.

Besides other projects, presently, CAP is working on the Phirangi nala issue. The nala is a heritage structure because it was constructed 200 years ago as a feeder channel to Himayathsagar from Chevella. It feeds 40 minor irrigation sources (tanks) to stabilise about 8,000 acres of land for 55 villages. However, it is not filling these tanks because

---

[70] February 6, 1991, The New York Times
[71] Rajesh (2000). Urban mismanagement blamed for killer Indian flood. 28th August 2000.
[72] September 16th 2005 The Hindu

it is encroached and illegal construction activities are taking place. The local struggle committee highlighting this issue is known as committee for protection of Phirangi Nala. CAP and the local struggle committee were successful in bringing the issue to the notice of the State Human Rights Commission. The Commission criticised the Ranga Reddy Collector for not initiating action to curb encroachments along the nala's path despite its frequent directions to do so. The Collector has issued an order to arrest the violators.

As an association, the *Save Lake Mission* is an initiative undertaken by Dr. Reddy wherein he along with the *Indian Association of Aquatic Biologist* has worked towards saving the lakes in and around Hyderabad from pollution. Dr. Reddy is appointed by the High Court of Andhra Pradesh as Member of Expert Committee to prepare an action plan to protect Saroornagar Lake.[73]

5.2.10 Citizens for Better Public Transport in Hyderabad (CBPTH)

Citizens for Better Public Transport in Hyderabad is a coalition of about 50 civil society organisations and individuals who would like to generate a public debate and involve the civil society on the options for public transportation in Hyderabad.

In a Citizen Declaration for Better Public Transport in Hyderabad (march 2007), CBPTH demanded that a number of measures are to be implemented as a package with a strong political will to reduce congestion, "save peoples' time and money", improve air quality, and promote public health by making public transportation a comfortable and dignified experience for citizens in Hyderabad. CBPTH believes that a metropolitan transport authority with representatives from the concerned departments, peoples' representatives and civil society should be constituted. It should be the policy making body for public transport in the city. Furthermore, CBPTH demands improvement in public transport infrastructure, pedestrian pathways all along the roads and zebra crossings at all intersections and bus stops. There should be no road without a footpath. In the charter, CBPTH also demanded that dedicated bus lanes should be provided on important roads. Also taken into account is the fact that Hyderabad lacks a strong well trained and well paid traffic police personnel.

CBPTH is one of the few voices which has consistently questioned the governments' decision on building an elevated metro rail track in Hyderabad rather than putting efforts in the improvement of the existing MMTS (Multi Modal Transit System) by taking up phase II of MMTS. MMTS trains are becoming popular with the Phase-I carrying

---

[73] Information gathered through personal interview of Dr. K Purusotham Reddy, articles in newspapers and magazines.

about 1.2 lakh passenger each day. The convener of CBPTH, Dr. C Ramachandraiah, has expressed severe reservations on various aspects related to the metro rail project in Hyderabad. The Hyderabad metro rail corridors are going to deface about 27 of the 137 listed heritage precincts of the city. Further, they are also going to affect about 44 buildings that are identified as having potential heritage value. The noise level that may be generated by an elevated metro rail would seriously hamper the peace of residential areas, schools and hospitals. The Environment and Social Impact Assessment (E&SIA) Report for Lines-1 and Lines-2 carried out in June 2003 are known to have used outdated methods, made unsubstantiated averments, neither studied the environment impact nor complied with the guidelines of the United Nations Environment Programme or Ministry of Environment and Forests (MOEF), Government of India. Civil society organisations like the United Federation of Resident Welfare Associations, SCOTRWA, Forum for A Better Hyderabad, PUCAAR, COVA, Gamana, Sannihita, CHATRI, Jana Vignana Vedika, Human Rights Forum etc. are working together to make the public aware of the above mentioned issues. They hold silent demonstrations, workshops, debates and discussions to generate awareness among the public and influence the policy makers. Dr. C. Ramachandraiah and O.M Dibara of Forum for Better Hyderabad have also filed a writ petition challenging the action of the State Government in going ahead with Hyderabad Metro Rail Project. The petitioners complained that the elevated Metro Rail would be passing adjacent to Secretariat and Assembly buildings posing great danger in the light of Maoist and ISI (Inter Services Intelligence, Pakistan) related extremist's activities in the State. Another complaint was that one of the alignments would be cutting across Hussain Sagar Lake in violation of the earlier judgement and with no rehabilitation plan or traffic management plan.

CBPTH believes that the inevitability of metro rail and providing "world class transport" to public in Hyderabad, while simultaneously weakening the existing public transport systems, has been carefully orchestrated in the last few years. CBPTH is demanding a public transport system, which will suit Hyderabad's specific characteristics in terms of the high density of population, road network, location of buildings on main roads, high prevalence of informal activities etc.

CBPTH is one of the very few networks working in the area of transport in Hyderabad. According to their own statement, the inherent honesty of the people associated with the network is its biggest strength. They are all committed towards building a more inclusive city of Hyderabad. All the activists consistently plan and carry out activities on a constant basis. Most of the findings highlighted by the network are based on research of the facts due to which the credibility of these findings is quiet high among the media and the public. CBPTH activists have a very good understanding of the geography of the city. This has helped them in suggesting more environment friendly as well as people friendly public transport system options. CBPTH has also been successful in disclosing the connection between political parties and the real estate sector in the state. It has gained media attention and the public's confidence through its persistent exposure of non-transparency in the Metro Rail deal. The High Court of the State of Andhra Pradesh has recognised the gravity of the matter and admitted the case instead of dismissing it.

One of the important drawbacks of CBPTH is that there are very few committed activists associated with the cause. Most of them are unable to give top priority to the activities of the organisation. Another big disappointment for CBPTH has been the attitude of various political parties in the state. After their initial attendance at a speaker's session none of the parties have shown any interest in taking up the cause. Even after the Satyam debacle and the plight of Maytas came into light, the political parties in the state have kept mum. According to CBPT, this reflects the sad state of affairs of the state.[74]

It is interesting to note, that the argumentation for a better public transport does not primarily originate from an environmental argumentation, but rather from a social and aesthetic point of view, i.e. public transport has to be made accessible to all and it has to be more comfortable and faster. Of course, the high cost of the Metro Rail project is one major argument against the project. However, the different possibilities of public transport systems suggested by CBPTH (MMTS, Bus Rapid Transit System) are not directly compared with the Metro Rail project regarding their environmental impact.

5.2.11 Forum for a Better Hyderabad

Forum for a Better Hyderabad is a local CSO concerned with environmental and cultural heritage issues. It has been the only environmental organisation to be accepted, even though in a very limited sense, by the authorities of Hyderabad as a partner in governance. It is also an environmental organisation that is both highly organised and has been active to a great extend. The three main objectives of FORUM today are to act constructively and proactively, to mobilise public opinion, and to speak loudly in a unified voice where transparency is lacking or where there is a lack of adequate

---

[74] Information gathered through personal interview with Dr. C Ramachandraiah, online research, pamphlets published by CBPTH, Economic and Political Weekly.

consideration of environmental issues by decision makers. Their primary message is that improper planning and lack of adequate impact assessments have had, and are still having, unnecessarily adverse ecological as well as economic consequences.

Although the results of victories may be not always be what the Forum's members had hoped for, they nonetheless continue fighting. It is partially because of this perseverance that Forum has gained a unique standing in the bureaucratic decision-making structure of Hyderabad. One of the members of Forum has served on the APPCB's (Andhra Pradesh Pollution Control Board) eight-member Consent for Establishment Committee, which grants permissions to industrial businesses in greater Hyderabad. Additionally, this same person sits on the APPCBs Monitoring Committee, which is charged with keeping track of industries' environmental records. Forum could thus influence the industrial business in the area.[75]

5.2.12 Society for Energy, Environment and Development (SEED)

Society for Energy, Environment and Development was formed in 1987 by a few professionals with expertise in Engineering, Management, Solar Energy, Law and Social Work. The purpose of this NGO is to draw upon the expertise of these professionals to create awareness about the Environment and Energy issues. It also aims at creating devices to enhance the quality of life. It promotes community development activities under a four-fold programme of employment, self-help, health and education.

The president of SEED is Dr. V. Bakthavatsalam, formerly Managing Director of Indian Renewable Energy Development Agency Limited (IREDA), New Delhi and a renowned renewable energy technologist. Founder & General Secretary is Prof M. Ramakrishna Rao, Ph.D., former Professor at the Indian Institute of Science, Bangalore.

SEED has invented a Solar Powered Solar Air Dryer for Solar Food Processing which is a novel and unique technology for dehydrating fruits, vegetables, forest produce, spices, and sea-food to the permissible moisture limits for better preservation, long shelf life and to the international cleanliness standards. This process can be accomplished by using solar dryers, which operate with zero energy cost and also preserve the nutrients in the food products. To guarantee high quality products through solar food processing, SEED has a well-equipped laboratory, with well-qualified staff maintaining quality and nutritional values.

---

[75] All of the information presented here about the Forum was taken from personal interviews and from the organisation's website: www.hyderabadgreens.org.

SEED organised 40 workshops in Andhra Pradesh and 20 training programmes for women and youth, covering 1,000 trainers and entrepreneurs and installed 130 solar dryers (demonstration and commercial models) in 12 states in India. The Department of Science and Technology, has selected SEED as a role model of a Science & Technology based NGO and rewarded core support with financial assistance for five years to strengthen its infrastructure, manpower, the equipment for training, library and adoptive research and development. The Ministry of New and Renewable Energy (MNRE) recognised the innovative and unique technology of SEED solar dryer and sanctioned 50 % subsidy on the cost of the dryer system from October, 2008 to entrepreneurs. This has led to an increase in the activity of solar food processing using solar dryer technology among micro-enterprises. The new solar micro enterprises have extended the processing from green leafy vegetables to marine foods.

Through its solar dryers, SEED has triggered the use of solar food processing technology. It has assigned the task of a solar dryer manufacture to fabricators, who produce it according to the specifications of SEED. It is now working on the technology to produce more efficient solar dryers.

According to Prof. Rao, SEED is doing pioneer work in the field of solar food processing technology. The use of environment friendly and zero cost solar energy in food processing will help the entrepreneurs from economically weak background to start small-scale food processing units. Thus, it can increase self-employment opportunities. The Solar dryers have found widespread use in rural areas in micro enterprises.

According to Prof. Rao, there is a lack of demand for products, which are processed by using solar dryers, and there are no proper business development strategies. The demand for these products, like fruit bars, dried vegetables etc., would have to be increased by attracting people to consume such products. This in turn would create demand for more micro-enterprises to produce solar heat dried products.[76]

5.2.13 Forum for Sustainable Development (FSD)

The Forum for Sustainable Development, Hyderabad, is a registered society. The affairs of FSD are managed by the Executive Committee, elected by the General Body. The total membership is around 50 and is open to all of those who want to work towards a sustainable development. By forging close ties with stakeholders in all aspects of its work,

---

[76] Information gathered through a visit to SEED laboratory, interview with Prof. Ramakrishna Rao, pamphlets published by SEED and short films made by SEED for promotional aspect. Most of the information is gathered from official SEED website www.seedngo.com (as directed by the founder secretary).

the FSD hopes to expand its reach and help more effectively to achieve sustainability. Its aims and objectives are:

- Advocacy of sustainable development by highlighting the social, economic and ecological impacts of environmental problems likely to be created by the developmental activities undertaken without proper appraisal and assessment.

- To create public awareness, to build informed public support, and pressure through democratic means, so as to influence the policy & decision makers to provide good governance, which alone can ensure sustainable development by minimising/eliminating inequalities, promoting people centric social order, protecting and improving environment etc.

- To act as a vehicle to circulate / disseminate information, to create public awareness of their Rights and Responsibilities and to provide a platform for public debates.

For example, FSD is actively associated with the protection of lake bodies in Hyderabad. In violation of water bodies' conservation provisions of Water, Land and Trees Act and HUDA notification on protection of lakes, the Andhra Pradesh Industrial Infrastructure Corporation (APIIC) has built a road in Durgam Cheruvu lake bed as part of its Hyderabad Knowledge City project. The project being developed on a 100 acre-site adjacent to the lake has a road that intrudes into the 30-meter buffer zone and the Full Tank Level mark of the lake. The Forum for Sustainable Development (FSD) and The Citizens Coalition for Saving Lakes in Hyderabad (CCSLH) protested against the APIIC move and said it violated different guidelines aimed at conserving city water bodies. 80 % of all lakes in Hyderabad are encroached, polluted or disappear in the course of time. The civic groups wanted HUDA to mark Full Tank Level and buffer zone boundaries and act against the organisations and individuals crossing the limit.[77] FSD also works in the area of GM crops and has highlighted the ills of corporatization of agriculture. It submitted a letter to the Prime Minister on April 16th, 2008 highlighting the problems associated with GM crops. FSD believes that GM technology threatens biodiversity and intensifies farmers' dependence on genetically modified seeds. On the other hand, "intellectual property rights" conflict directly with the age-old rights of farmers to produce, share or store seeds.

Furthermore, FSD has advocated for more transparency and public debate with regard to the Metro Rail project in Hyderabad. It has submitted a letter to the Managing

---

[77] July 6th 2008 The Hindu.

Director, Hyderabad Metro Rail Limited, in April 2008 highlighting its apprehensions regarding the project. As a response, an interactive session took place on May 10th 2008 with Mr. N.V.S. Reddy, Managing Director of Hyderabad Metro Rail. Several members of different NGOs in Hyderabad participated in this session. Queries posed by participants were concerning the economic viability of Hyderabad Metro Rail Project, the unimportance of MMTS phase 2, connectivity and common ticket facility (APSRTC and MMTS/MRTS) as well as provision for future expansion. FSD believes that for Hyderabad Metropolitan Area, an energy efficient urban plan is needed which can minimise the need for intra-city commuting (demand suppression). This can be achieved by decongestion of city centres, development of self-supporting townships etc. The urban land use planning and its strict implementation are of vital importance.

FSD is working more in the area of advocacy. They believe that finding solutions to problems such as poverty must involve approaches, which also address other issues like environmental degradation, lack of access to health care and education, social & economic inequalities.

Forum for Sustainable Development is an organisation of people concerned about the environment working passionately for environment protection and spreading awareness among communities. The members of this CSO believe in basing their actions on concrete facts. Forum for Sustainable Hyderabad is also active in other parts of the state of Andhra Pradesh. Its association with other CSOs helps the organisation to reach grass root levels and work efficiently. According to Mr. Reddy, Forum for Sustainable Hyderabad will benefit more with an increase in its membership in the long run.

There are several cooperations with other NGOs such as Forum for Better Hyderabad, Save Rock Society, Forum for Better Suryapet, Forum for Better Vishakapatnam, Energy Conservation Mission, Gamana and Bird Watchers Society.[78]

5.2.14 The Society for Preservation of Environment and Quality of Life (SPEQL)

The Society for Preservation of Environment and Quality of Life (SPEQL) is one of the oldest CSOs actively working on social and/or environmental issues in Hyderabad. It was formed in April 1988 with the main idea of creating necessary awareness among the citizens to protect, preserve, maintain and harness the natural environment in a sustainable manner including flora and fauna, aesthetic surroundings, cultural, historical and architectural heritage. SPEQL is part of a number of agitations and legal activism

---

[78] Information gathered through consultation with Dr. Jeevananda Reddy, Secretary, FSD; articles in newspapers, pamphlets published by FSD and official website of FSD www.fsdhyd.org.

for the protection of the lakes in Hyderabad, to ban plastic carry bags, noise pollution, and bio-medical waste disposal among others. It has around 200 members.

The "Quality of Life" basically depends on the "Environment" in which we live and the depletion of natural resources leads to degradation of environment. The focus areas of SPEQL are the following:

- Urban solid waste management
- Treatment and Disposal of Industrial Waste and Sewerage
- Conservation of energy and Water by good demand management
- To create/organise mass movement for control of air, noise pollution and particularly in urban areas.
- To create awareness in observing traffic rules and discipline.
- Protection and preservation of water bodies, lakes and underground water.
- Efficient mass transport system in urban areas.
- To identify and protect waste land, vacant government land for development of public parks and play grounds with the cooperation and help of local authorities.
- To promote urban forestry and prevent deforestation.
- To evolve the concept of harmonious development that will ensure sustainable and balanced growth of both urban and rural areas so as to prevent migration of rural population to urban areas.
- To take up Public Interest Litigation on issues like illegal occupation of government lands, illegal buildings construction, high rise structures, indiscriminate and frequent changes in zoning regulations such as land use, disposal of government lands, etc. affecting the environment and quality of life of the present and future generations.

Within the last years, SPEQL has conducted many initiatives and activities aiming at raising environmental awareness of the citizens of Hyderabad.

SPEQL has set up a pilot vermin culture project in the fruit market of Gaddinannaram in LB Nagar, making use of biodegradable waste generated by the market yard in April 1996. The entire process took about eight months from the date of taking over the land to commissioning the project to get the vermin compost from the first batch of 20 beds ready for marketing by November 1996. On the spot training to farmers was also given.

In 2005, the vermin culture project was shifted to NTR Nagar vegetable market. The project came to an end in 2007.

In 2002, the Institution of Engineers (India), Andhra Pradesh State Centre and Society for Preservation of Environment and Quality of Life (SPEQL) organised a Round Table Conference on "Traffic Problems in Twin Cities - Short Term Solutions", in association with Hyderabad City Traffic Police. Representatives from Town Planning Department, Andhra Pradesh State Road Transport Corporation, Jawaharlal Nehru Technological University, SPEQL, Hyderabad City Traffic Police, and Auto Drivers Union took active part in the deliberations and came up with suggestions on short-term solutions for the traffic problem in Hyderabad.

SPEQL had also opposed mega tourism projects involving several concrete structures around the Hussain Sagar lake like amusement park, open air theatre, State Museum, food courts, music and laser shows as this will have a disastrous effect on the already fragile eco-system of the vastly shrunk lake, add to congestion and push down the per capita recreational space in the Municipal Corporation of Hyderabad area from the meagre $0.5\,m^2$ at present to a new low. Despite the green and clean campaigns, Hyderabad's figure is poor compared to the national average of three m^2 per head. SPEQL contends that these projects, involving conversion of adjoining parks, have been planned without the mandatory Environmental Impact Assessment and Public Hearing, violate the Master Plan and Zonal Development Plans governing the land use pattern, as also the orders of the Supreme Court and the High Court of Andhra Pradesh.[79]

SPEQL has also questioned the government's move in handing over notified areas to private parties depriving the birds of their natural environment. As a result different species of birds have disappeared into the wild or facing extinction. SPEQL has been highlighting the helplessness of a community whose rights to clean air and water are violated. It has also brought into focus the irreversible threat to urban environment caused by the mushrooming growth of illegally constructed buildings.

As one of the oldest NGOs in Hyderabad, SPEQL has done pioneering work in many areas and has set the trail ablaze for others to follow. It has campaigned against several issues and has expressed its opinions based on authentic facts. For example, it questioned the government's move in handing over notified areas to private parties depriving the birds of their natural environment. As a result, sparrows, crows, pigeons, parrots, and dozens of other common birds have disappeared into the wild or are facing extinction.

---

[79] May 17, 2000 The Hindu.

But due to rapid urbanisation and indifferent attitude of the administration it is hard to make any sane opinion heard.

The SPEQL has a vast number of cooperation partners in and around Hyderabad. Those include Forum for Better Hyderabad, Indian National Trust for Art and Cultural Heritage, Institution of Engineers, Administrative Staff College of India, Salarjung Museum, Historical Society of Hyderabad and the Centre for Deccan Studies.[80]

5.2.15 Energy Conservation Mission (ECM)

Following its motto: "It is the duty of every citizen, who holds the earth's energy resources as a trustee, to utilise the same, in such a way, that a better environment, is left behind, for future generations", the ECM promotes energy conservation awareness through functional groups for various sectors- Domestic, Industry, Agricultural, Commercial, Transportation, Educational Institutions, Renewable Sources of Energy, Standards & Labelling etc. Energy Savers Clubs and several awareness programmes were established in some of the Industrial Areas, Schools and Colleges, with the idea of promoting energy efficient practices and technologies in the industry and creating awareness among students, teachers and professors. In the last years, ECM was actively involved in the "National Energy Conservation Week" and organised exhibitions titled "Save Energy 2004" and "Save Energy 2005" to present energy efficient products, technologies and the potential of renewable energy sources. It has also organised Round Table Discussions and Interactive Sessions on Energy Efficient Building Codes, Energy Management, Energy Efficient Lighting Systems and Solar-powered LED Lamps, Evaluation of the energy efficiency of agriculture pump sets, Bio-Fuels and Solar Water Heating Systems and others.

The ECM Action Plan for 2009 includes the organisation of the National Energy Conservation Week from 14th to 20th December 2009, another Save Energy 2009 Exhibition and All India Seminar in October / November, 2009, further awareness programmes in schools and colleges and more involvement of the commercial sector as well as Residential Welfare Societies.[81]

---

[80] Information gathered through consultation with Mrs. Anuradha Reddy, President SPEQL; articles in newspapers and journals.

[81] Information taken from ECM's website: www.save-today-survive-tomorrow.com.

5.2.16 Confederation of Voluntary Organisations (COVA)

COVA is a national network of over 800 organisations working for the vision of communal harmony, peace and social justice. COVA works with women, children, youth and men from different sections and communities on the issues of communal harmony, women's empowerment, child rights, youth advancement, education, health, environment and civic amenities. Apart from working with the poor, COVA also actively works with the educated and professional classes to enlist their support and involvement for social transformation through college discussion groups and professional club gatherings. COVA believes that involving people from different communities in development programs is an effective way of achieving communal harmony and national integration. Hence, COVA ensures that all its member organisations involve people from different communities in their programs. In order to achieve its mandate, COVA undertakes programs at the grassroots, networking of organisations and institutions, research, training, advocacy and policy interventions. COVA also works in alliance with a number of international organisations to promote peace in India and across the globe.

In its General Body, the Governing Body as well as the Managing Committee representatives of Muslim and Non-Muslim communities, as well as males and females are equally appointed.

COVA is an NGO designed to support the Muslim minority in India as there are many programmes supporting other backward communities such as Dalits or tribal communities, but only a few working for the empowerment of Muslim communities. Therefore COVA works with the population of the old city of Hyderabad through initiatives for economic empowerment for women, children's and youth programmes as well as civic rights and advocacy programmes.

There are several peace-measures concerning social harmony taken. Those include, for instance, riot control, communal harmony programmes such as service during different processions or joint celebration of festivals, sambandh[82] and interfaith forums to secure the communal peace of the area concerned.

The most recent activities of COVA can be stated as follows:

- COVA participated in the first historical Delhi-Multan peace march that began in Delhi on 23rd March 2005 (Bhagat Singh's Martyrdom Day) and concluded in Multan on 11th May 2005 (the day India conducted nuclear tests at Pokhran).

---

[82] Sambandh, an annual event of inter-school and inter-collegiate competitions is organised from 6th to 8th August to commemorate nuclear holocaust at Hiroshima and Nagasaki. Students from schools and colleges across the city participate in the competitions.

- Representatives of COVA and PIPFPD (Pakistan-India Peoples' Forum for Peace and Democracy) - Andhra Pradesh chapter celebrated the 10th Anniversary of PIPFPD held at Lahore, Pakistan on 4th and 5th September 2004. Dr Irfan Basha from COVA presented a research paper on the "Socio-economic Status of Muslims in India" at the meeting of the Joint Committee of Minorities of the Forum.

- COVA took active role in collaboration with other civil society organisations, unions and social activists in organising an "Anti-War Assembly" in Hyderabad from 17th to 19th December 2004. Anti-war international as well as national activists participated in this Assembly.

- COVA's strategy of creating inter-community developmental alliances through the city and district level networks effectively integrated the communal and social harmony agenda with the development agenda. COVA works in cooperation with other organisations at the (Hyderabad) city, state, national and international level to promote peace and justice.

- At the State level, COVA collaborated in the launch of Social Watch Report focusing on food, education, health and water on 27th October 2003. On this occasion, Andhra Pradesh Social Watch was initiated. Other organisations collaborating in this process are: Centre for World Solidarity, Centre for Environmental Concerns, Dappu Collective, Samata, Coalition for Peace and Harmony, Anveshi and others.

- COVA is also a member of the AP Alliance for Child Rights and AP Child Rights Advocacy Forum, the Voluntary Action Network (VANI) (the Director of COVA is a member of the Working Committee of VANI), the Coalition for Nuclear Disarmament and Peace (CNDP) and is the secretariat of the Andhra Pradesh Chapter of Pakistan India People's Forum for Peace and Democracy (PIPFPD). COVA is also represented in government committees such as the planning commission and the AP GO-NGO Co-ordination Committee.[83]

5.2.17 People's Union for Civic Action and Rights (PUCAAR)

People's Union for Civic Action and Rights is the result of the efforts of COVA to evolve a suitable model that enables marginalised communities to adopt rights based approach for claiming basic services and amenities as a matter of basic citizenship rights. Over a hundred basti[84] meetings were held with different sections of society participating in

---

[83] Information taken from website www.covanetwork.org.
[84] Basti: slums or shantytown.

six mandals of the old city, namely, Charminar, Bandlaguda, Bahadurpura, Saidabad, Golconda, and Asif Nagar to get comprehensive data on civic amenities and other social issues. Important issues that emerged out of these meetings were shared with intellectuals and activists. The People's Manifesto was released during election time at a public meeting at Charminar, Hyderabad, on 18th February 2004 to make political parties aware of real issues affecting people in the old city.

2009 being an election year a "People's Manifesto", a charter of demands for the overall development of the old city was released on Feb. 8th. After its release the manifesto was also handed over to representatives of various political parties for inclusion into their respective manifestos for the upcoming elections. It was prepared by holding a series of workshops and basti-level meetings with a cross section of people of old city. PUCAAR had organised three workshops in January this year in which social activists, community leaders, students, women leaders, academicians and educationists participated to hammer out the demands for the manifesto. All the issues that are afflicting the public of old city including housing, civic amenities, lack of welfare programmes, education, public utility services, recreational spaces, electricity problems, drainage issues, law and order problems have been included in the manifesto. The PUCAAR officials informed that the charter of demands would be a part of a larger process of All India People's Manifesto led by national-level campaign Wada Na Todo Abhiyan (WINTA) formed to monitor the progress made by government of India on its promises in the National Common Minimum Programme (NICMP).[85]

Activities so far:

- Voter Awareness Programmes in the bastis.
- Open Forums before the general elections, to which each candidate contesting to the A.P. Legislative Assembly was invited to interact with the people of the constituency.
- Education Campaign, in which a survey was conducted on the existing facilities in 337 government schools in the old city of Hyderabad, 25 thousand signatures were collected demanding improvement of these schools, and submitted memorandums to the Ministers and officials concerned and the Chief Minister Dr Y.S. Raja Sekhar Reddy. As a result the government sanctioned Rs. 5 crores[86] to improve the condition of government schools in the old city.

---

[85] Feb 9th 2009, The Hindu
[86] One crore equals 10,000,000 Rupees.

- Basti Committees in twelve bastis
- Training programs for the Basti Committee members in collaboration with National Centre for Advocacy Studies, Pune.
- Redress of civic issues like drainage systems, road repairs, drinking water supply and garbage clearance in the bastis.
- Awareness programs on consumer rights, human rights and Right to Information.
- Monitoring of distribution of ration cards in the old city of Hyderabad

PUCAAR has also been able to facilitate a slow but distinct shift in the political agenda of the old city of Hyderabad from that of communal to issues of development. This is contributing towards improving access to civic amenities by the poor and marginalised sections of society living in these areas.

PUCAAR along with other citizen organisations has also filed a complaint seeking stoppage of the 'unauthorised' construction activity taken up by the Hyderabad Golf Association within the walls of the Naya Qila (Golconda fort – a heritage monument) encompassing an area of 50 acres.[87]

PUCAAR is playing an important role in spreading awareness among the poor and marginalised sections of the society about their right to basic services. It is performing an important function (by making use of bottom-up approach) within the society by helping the marginalised sections to participate in the democratic process with dignity. Peoples' involvement in large numbers in solving the issues is perceived as the strength of PUCAAR. Even though there are only four frequent members, they get a number of volunteers from the different mandals.

PUCAAR is working hard towards making people aware of their basic rights. It is educating people and spreading awareness among the marginalised communities due to which people are now demanding better facilities from the administration. The attitude of the administration towards these marginalised communities is now changing due to PUCAAR's initiatives. These people who at one time were reluctant to approach the government officials for fear of being turned away are now demanding services which are their basic rights. This attitudinal change is the biggest boost any democratic society can get. PUCAAR facilitated the survey visit of the team of Andhra Pradesh election watch to one of the slums near Dabeerpura to find out the missing and fake names, if any, in the voters list on March 21st 2009. These kinds of activities are making the people as well as the government officials take notice of PUCAAR's agenda.

---

[87] Nov 7th 2008, The Hindu

According to PUCAAR, between 2004 and 2009 nothing much positive has come out in the broad political environment. The Right to Information Act 2005 and the protection of women from domestic violence act 2005 are two positive steps ensuring transparency and security. But at the same time the Special Economic Zones act 2005 was promulgated. Thousand of acres of land have been surrendered to corporate houses often displacing hapless farmers and labourers. In spite of large amount of funds made available to state governments under Sarva Siksha Abhiyan, Jawaharlal Nehru Nation Urban Renewal mission (JNNURM) and other schemes, unfortunately PUCAAR has not found much to change in the charter of demands made in the people's manifesto of 2004 on the eve of general elections again in 2009.

PUCAAR's cooperation partners include People's Initiative Network, Forum for better Hyderabad, Chhatri and the Right to Walk Foundation.[88]

5.2.18 The United Federation for Residents' Welfare Association (UFERWAS)

The primary objective of UFERWAS is to bring together all independent resident welfare associations on a common platform for collective action. It is designed to help those citizens, who are frustrated by delays and broken promises of development from elected representatives, by advocating independence from 'middlemen' and taking up the developmental activities on its own. In UFERWAS members of different welfare associations have the opportunity to share with each other their experiences in their respective residential welfare associations and to discuss and develop strategies to solve problems through joint initiative.

The member associations of UFERWAS are trying at their level to change the existing culture of living in apartment complexes by bringing the families residing in the complexes together. So that, in emergencies, they can help each other instead of depending on authorities. They regularly organise meetings with local barbers, cable operators, suppliers of domestic needs, auto drivers and domestic helps. The federation initiates interaction between citizens and the police, plans as well to invite representatives from schools for interaction. Thereby, they want to avoid problems in the colony and maintain a peaceful atmosphere in the neighbourhood. From handling mosquito menace to development of parks and checking the quality standards of eateries, the federation is all set to solve its problems on its own.

On 1st March 2009 Dr. Rao, V. B. J. Chelikani (President, Standing Committee of Tarnaka Residents Welfare Association) took over as the president of UFERWAS. Its

---

[88] Information taken from www.covanetwork.org/pucaar.htm unless otherwise stated.

Executive Vice Presidents are V. Gopal Rao, G. V. Rao, P. Anji Reddy, K. R. C. Reddy, T. Satyanarayana and B. T. Srinivasan.

The formation of UFERWAS is a unique initiative, which motivates residents to take a proactive role in the development of their area. In the course of monthly meetings, the problems are brought to its notice. UFERWAS, in turn, brings them to the notice of the concerned officials in GHMC. Each volunteer or member of the Federation is in charge of a different cell such as Education, Sanitation and Health, Engineering (which covers roads and buildings), Town Planning, Horticulture, Senior Citizens Cell, etc.

A weakness of it is the lack of concern by many citizens. Except a handful of people, the majority of citizens are generally apathetic and not responsive. Generally they act only when they are personally involved or attend the meetings only when they have a problem. They do not evince interest to address others' problems.[89]

5.2.19 Tarnaka Residents' Welfare Association

The Tarnaka Resident's Welfare Associations is a nationally as well as internationally notable community concept which is–disappointed due to a lack of political mediation through representation at the level of urban governance–trying to find new forms of self-management and development within its small range of community level. The Resident's Welfare Association builds the core of social consensus and is also well aware of all the diversity that exists in the local community. An informal but well-structured Ward Sabha, comparable to the Gram Sabha at village level, is regularly held and represents the TRWA's expression of direct democracy. The Ward Sabha adopts a micro-plan for the area's development and can, if necessary, serve as a tool of moral recall of the political representatives. The TRWA formed an informal Ward Committee composed of all resident's welfare associations and the government corporator as the ex-official chairperson. This Ward committee meets once a month to solve everyday problems and follow the micro-plan designed by the Ward Sabha. Before convening the Ward Sabha, the population of the ward is handed out a questionnaire aiming at identifying the major concerns of the residents. A team of experts is then asked to formulate a new micro-plan, time frame and distribute responsibilities on the basis of the outcomes. Within these considerations, local level executive officials of different departments are invited to participate and enrich the debates by technical insight information. Another outstanding aspect of the TRWA is the one of community building. Due to the social

---

[89] Information gathered from a personal interview with Mr Rao Chelikani and several articles: The Hindu, March 2nd, 2009, and The Hindu, March 2nd, 2009.

diversity and often conflicting private parties and minorities, the Standing Committee of Tarnaka Resident's Welfare Associations (SCOTRWA) is trying to ease the tension by forming formal and informal vertical associations like the resident's welfare associations, horizontal associations of consumers, children and senior citizens as well as professional associations of the dhobis (launderer), domestic workers, lawyers or doctors. Theses associations are brought together in order to reconcile them through mediation by dialogue and mutual help. Another, not yet fully visible idea is the idea of Flat Culture. This is a concept aimed at transforming the many different parties of an apartment-complex into one extended joint family network by e.g. promoting car sharing, centralised buying and so forth.[90]

Regarding the activities and strategies of the TRWA, there is an insufficiency of motivated volunteers to improve direct communication, to facilitate, and to educate the residents in social mobilisation. Whenever they have an individual problem, residents come searching for the SCOTRWA members, uninhibited by the fact that they have never participated in any common activity before. Often there is resignation among the people about their inability to change anything, due also to the fact that past efforts have not shown the maximum expected results. The TRWA faces managerial problems in mobilising people, as nobody thinks it possible either to change or improve the communication techniques or to refine the tools to inform people differently. The tools that are being used at present are not efficient, badly maintained, or poorly utilised.

Furthermore, the members of SCOTRWA do not yet conceive management of the organisation as a matter of balancing their problems and solutions, their resources and their needs. They rather still think in terms of power-relations, influencing the government, political or party affiliations, personal friendships, caste or religion to get things accomplished. Inherent worth of the matter, merit, rules and regulations, rule of law, due procedures, objective criteria for taking decisions, etc. are not sufficiently trusted by them as well as the public at large. They think others do not respect those values and they justify their management-by-manipulation on this assumption.[91]

---

[90] Information taken from SCOTRWA's pamphlet (2009).
[91] See Pilot Project Report No 6, Interviews with SCOTRWA members.

6 Development of Communication and Participation Strategies

Participative and communicative approaches are essential to create and increase awareness for the consequences of climate change and mitigation- and adaptation strategies among affected stakeholders while integrating the local knowledge and the needs of the affected groups and activating them to take self-initiative. Communication represents an important constituent of action.[92] Strategies for reducing poverty, for example, are more successful, if they involve communication strategies. The same applies to climate change and energy efficiency that necessitate new forms of communication and participation.[93] These consist in an intensive discussion on the reasons and consequences of climate change, which is not only oriented at political solutions, but also includes possibilities of self-action and change of daily routines.

Thus, the communication and participation strategy of the project takes two approaches to communication and participation, for which different methods and instruments have to be used. One approach is to foster dialogue and cooperation between the stakeholders of different sectors, i.e. public authorities, the business sector and the CSOs, as well as among the CSOs themselves. This can be done, e.g. through a scenario process, future workshops, strategic workshops, stakeholder conferences, round tables etc.

On the other hand, the communication and participation strategies are directed at the individual level, the citizens themselves (not their representatives), as mitigation- and adaptation strategies include individual action and change of behaviour and daily routines. Individuals as consumers demand for resources, both direct (at home or on the road) and indirect (mediated by globalising production-consumption chains), and thus contribute to CO_2 emissions and climate change. At the individual level participative and communicative methods include awareness raising (e.g. films, homepage), knowledge generation, activating methods (e.g. citizens' exhibition, spatial partnerships, future workshops), but also methods to enhance political legitimacy (e.g. planning cells / citizens juries).

The analysis in this study implies, though, that approaches used in Germany or Europe cannot be transferred directly to the Indian context without adaptation. An exclusively ecocentric approach (borrowed from western movements) may not suit to India, as the

---

[92] McDonnell, OECD (2006)
[93] Walk (2007)

main concerns here continue to be basic needs. Looking at participation in India means taking a stand against eurocentrism and seeking a specifically Indian definition of 'stakeholder engagement' and 'bottom-up' processes.

6.1 Stakeholder Dialogue and Cooperation

The analysis during the project activities has enriched our knowledge about the existing and predicted problems of sustainability in an emerging megacity: Communication and participation of civil society have to be integrated as key elements of project activities. Civil society organisations play a key role in action research directed towards empowerment, citizen's engagement and participative urban planning and governance. But the analysis also revealed a lack of transparent information and lack of cooperation of public authorities with civil society as well as high levels of corruption as problems. These are also main causes of political distrust. Although some politicians, planners and other decision makers believe that citizens' participation is necessary to make efforts towards a more sustainable development in Hyderabad successful, the cooperation between civil society and government/public authorities seems to be less harmonious than, for example, in Germany. In many political decision-making or planning processes citizens' participation is seen as an obstacle or drawback, especially when planning in short-term perspectives. The long-term profits like transparency, activation and legitimacy are often not seen. But as sustainable development and climate protection have to be also seen in a long-term perspective, participation–especially on the local level–has to be strengthened. Citizens do want to take part in decision making processes and influence development, as can be seen by the examples of different civil society movements for environmental causes, transparency and accountability and the growing number of CSOs in general.

Furthermore, at least in the case of Hyderabad, there is little cooperation between the business sector and CSOs, although some Indian companies have a reputation of financing and supporting environmental, developmental and social projects (e.g. TATA, Bajaj and Mafatlal).[94] Therefore, communication and participation strategies as well as capacity-building measures have to be developed that strengthen the cooperation between the different sectors, namely civil society, government and business sector. An important task here is to foster communication and cooperation by promoting dialogue and to take up and implement actionable research by policymakers, CSOs, and other

---

[94] Kuhn (2006)

actors. These methods should include the networking and cooperation among CSOs from different levels (e.g. Community Based Organisations and Content Based Organisations, local and national CSOs), which needs to be strengthened. To assure this, processes like communication, participation and cooperation management are firmly integrated in the project structure of the overall project. This is especially important, as one main task of the project is to secure the adoption of the Perspective Action Plan by politicians, agencies, groups and firms.

The stakeholder dialogue and stakeholder cooperation will be organised in the form of participatory workshops (e.g. scenario process and planning/future workshops) and meetings according to the following planning circle: visioning (stakeholder identification and problem analysis, initial visioning and scenario building), strategising (select key scenario and related strategies, prioritise activities), planning (detailed plan(s) for concerted action developed, identify tasks and responsibilities, define information flows), implementing (activities implemented according to plans) and reflecting (lessons drawn out of preceding planning cycle, documenting processes, evaluation reports).

The actors relevant to the overall project have been identified by the project partners during the first phase of the project. Also, the scenario process has already been started with a joint scenario workshop of German and Indian partners: The scenario process builds the framework for the co-operation between the German and the Indian partners. Its aim is (1) to jointly initiate a successive process on scenario development for the Greater Hyderabad region. Scenarios can be used widely in order to understand different ways in which future events might unfold; (2) to educe descriptors relevant to possible city futures from the viewpoint of local committees, civil society representatives, scientists and public stakeholders in the fields of energy, transport, poverty, food and nutrition, lifestyles & consumption, natural resource management & environment, governance & institutions and surrounding conditions (population growth, global and national regulatory framework etc.); (3) to reduce these descriptors to the most important ones for mitigation and adaptation strategies (4) to work out linkages between the fields mentioned above; (5) to discuss possible futures for the Greater Hyderabad region 2025 ("worst-case scenario", "trend scenario", "best-case scenario"); (6) to discuss concepts, approaches and paths to reach the vision of sustainability; and in the long run (7) to develop a mutual vision for the Greater Hyderabad region in 2025. The scenario process will be carried forward throughout the project.

Furthermore, as an activity of stakeholder dialogue in the sector of traffic and transport, the conference "Hyderabad Citizens' Charter for Urban Transport" was organised on 21st of February 2009, in co-operation with the Goethe-Centre Hyderabad, Right to Walk Foundation and PTV. Participants and speakers from civil society organisations, professional organisations, transport corporations, government offices and universities participated in the conference. Its aim was to bring together the most important stakeholders from different levels in the field of transport and traffic in order to discuss the different interests and possible conflicts and to eventually formulate a charter for citizen-friendly traffic. As already mentioned, it was shown that the traffic problem is mainly perceived as a safety (e.g. low safety for pedestrians, too many accidents) and time problem (traffic jams and long commuting times), which has to be linked to the necessity of energy efficiency and mitigation. Subsequent to the conference, a Citizens' Charter with the demands of the attendants was formulated and handed over to public authorities and political parties.

6.2 Participation and Communication at the Citizens Level

Individuals as consumers demand for resources and thus contribute to CO_2 emissions and climate change. In the context of mitigation strategies for climate change the fast emerging middle-classes of countries with high economic growth pose a particularly important target group, as their rising demand for resources contributes substantially to climate change, biodiversity loss, acidification, air and water pollution. Therefore, the Residents' Welfare Associations are very important stakeholders for participative and communicative processes at the level of citizens, as they mainly represent middle-class communities.

On the one hand, the complexity of climate issues is a challenge for individuals. This implies that sufficient information and knowledge about relevant issues of energy and climate change is required for individuals to become more aware of the necessity of individual action. On the other hand, the activation of citizens is a matter of issue-framing, i.e. to motivate people to take action, the issues of climate change and mitigation have to be linked to issues that directly concern the people, e.g. matters of livelihood and development, as is shown in many studies (see Chapter 1). This has also been proven by our work so far in Hyderabad in the sector of transport and traffic. Therefore, the growing complexity of climate issues is a challenge for individuals not only in terms of understanding the problem, but also in terms of translating the information into local action and thereby fostering participative governance structures. This means that awareness raising, knowledge generating and activating methods are necessary.

Through different elements and levels of communication and participation, different effects can be achieved: Transparency of information and public awareness can be improved through different forms of presentation, e.g. visual elements like the documentary films or the homepage. (Social) Mobilisation can be achieved through activating participation methods like future workshops,[95] spatial partnerships and citizens' exhibitions. The latter are methods developed by nexus Institute for the European context[96] and have to be transferred to the context of Indian megacities. (Political) legitimacy for development plans can be reached through democratic methods for participative planning like citizens' juries (planning cells), where randomly selected citizens develop an advisory report for the government on a specific topic.[97]

On the individual level, different participative processes will be initiated in cooperation with the Indian and German project partners on the local level. Exemplary is the already initiated participative process in the field of traffic and transportation:

A major factor in producing greenhouse gas emissions in Hyderabad is the massive increase in motorised traffic. Therefore, one focal point of the project is to develop a sustainable, energy efficient transport management system with the participation of citizens and relevant stakeholders. The aim is to integrate the knowledge of citizens into the planning process, to analyse the citizens' awareness on problems in the transport sector and to develop innovative solutions that are supported by the local stakeholders. Does the transportation system meet the needs of Hyderabad's citizens? How can pollution be reduced and safety and energy-efficiency be increased at the same time? In co-operation with the main partner of nexus, the "Tarnaka Residents Welfare Association", a citizens' exhibition was organised in Tarnaka, a locality of Hyderabad city. As part of this exercise, in co-operation with PTV and TRWA, male/female citizens and representatives of the local administration in Tarnaka were interviewed to find out which problems they face in transportation and what kind of solutions suggest for a sustainable traffic and transportation. Out of the interviewees' statements and their pictures, a citizens' exhibition was designed in two languages (Telugu and English). It was inaugurated on March 1st, 2009 within the "5th Ward Sabha" (meeting) of the TRWA. A large number of residents from Tarnaka and Hyderabad and representatives from Osmania University, Hyderabad, and from Delhi were present. The citizens' exhibition is a participative method that visualises citizens' perspectives and presents them to a large group of people. Thus, it shall foster the dialogue between citizens, decision makers

---

[95] Jungk / Müllert (1987)
[96] See Schophaus / Dienel (2003)
[97] Dienel (2002); Reinert (1998)

and other stakeholders in the locality and in Hyderabad. The exhibition was on display until the middle of March 2009 in the community hall of Tarnaka and will be shown in further public buildings (e.g. other community halls, Jawaharlal Nehru Technological University, Osmania University and Goethe-Centre) to reach more people. The attention generated through the citizens' exhibition for the matter of sustainable traffic shall be utilised to develop new projects to reduce emissions in traffic until the 2010 milestone. As a next step, citizens' juries in different localities of Hyderabad on the topic of "The Future of Public Transport" or future workshops are planned in co-operation with the TRWA.

In addition, the interactive online-dialogue "Ready to Move–Towards energy efficient and climate friendly traffic and transport solutions", a further participative communication tool to develop solutions for a climate friendly and energy efficient traffic system in Hyderabad, was developed on the website of the project. It aims to activate as many citizens and actors from Hyderabad as possible to discuss about (1) their problems with the prevailing traffic conditions in Hyderabad, (2) their visions for a climate-friendly, energy efficient Hyderabad in the year 2020 and (3) feasible action strategies for a more sustainable traffic system with lower emission levels can be realised for Hyderabad. These ideas and the knowledge shall be incorporated in future planning processes of the project. After the completion of the online-dialogue the findings will be evaluated and presented to the local actors in Hyderabad for further discussion.

In the end, within the field of traffic and transportation, the project shall come up not only with practical results, but also with generalised strategies for transportation planning and for facing the challenges of climate change and energy security in the (local) transport sector.

Other examples where the organisation of participative processes, including both approaches (stakeholder dialogue and individual action), is intended are:

Socio-technical Experiments for Low-Emission Lifestyles:

- Participative Energy Management (with RESS / PIK): Technical and institutional aspects of energy efficiency improvement mean reduction through Energy-Technology Transition, change in behaviour and better management (Regulatory Reforms and Governance). These processes include bringing together the different stakeholders (firms, farmers, villagers, local officials) and also an awareness rising for renewable energies and a change in individual behaviour towards the use of renewable energies and the according technologies.

- Rural-urban linkages (with PIK): With instruments for rural-urban linkages ("Spatial Partnerships") we want to strengthen the socio-economic networks between Hyderabad and the surrounding Region.
- Community Radio: The aim of the Community Radio, organised in cooperation with the Tarnaka Residents Welfare Association, is to find out, if 'Community Radio' is accepted as a tool for Empowerment and Community Building.

The application of these communication and participation methods and the implementation of tools have to be designed as learning processes. According to Obser (2003), people have to be architects and engineers of concepts (concerning their environs) to achieve sustainable development. This is reflected in systematic participation, which means to integrate participation and communication concepts in the planning processes and the implementation of projects at all scales. Through the realisation of case studies and by supporting the other work packages in their communication and participation activities, Action Research Cycles get started. These research processes will eventually show, what kind of tools or methods are applicable for which purpose and target group and how they have to be adapted in order to work in a specific context of the megacity in India. The processes will be accompanied by further qualitative research methods. Literature reviews as well as the scientific exchange with partners from Universities in Hyderabad and finally a project monitoring ensure the quality of the results and findings.

References

BBC. 2007. "World Service Poll: All Countries Need To Take Major Steps on Climate Change: Global Poll." London.

Balan, P.P. 2006. "Grass Roots of Democracy: Revisiting the Grama Sabhas in Kerala." In *Decentralised Governance and Poverty Reduction: Lessons from Kerala*, eds. Balan, Ray Retna Raj, 130–141. Kerala Institute of Local Administration, Thrissur, India.

Center for Good Governance. 2006. "The Right to Information Act, 2005: A Guide for Civil Society Organisations." Available at: www.rti.org.in/Documents/Publications/CSO%20Guide.pdf

The Central Institute of Research and Training in Public. 1967. "Voluntary Service in India: A Study." New Delhi.

Centre for Civil Society. "Community Participation Law." CCS series on NURM Reforms No 2, New Delhi.

Chakrabarti, Dhar. 2002. "Urban Crisis in India: new initiatives for sustainable cities." In *Development and Cities: Essays from Development in Practice*, eds. Deborah Eade and David Westendorff. UK.

Dahiya, Bharat. 2000. "Democracy, Governance and Environmental Management in Contemporary Urban India." Edinburgh: Paper for *16th European Conference on Modern South Asian Studies*.

Dienel, Peter. 2002. "Die Planungszelle: Der Bürger als Chance." Wiesbaden.

Dembowski, Hans. 2001. "Taking the State to Court: Public Interest Litigation and Public Sphere in Metropolitan India." Asia House.

Dohrman, Jona, and Alexander Fischer. 2001. "Public Interest Litigation in Indien." In *Indien-Jahrbuch*, Institut für Asienkunde Hamburg. Available at: http://www.diz-ev.de/PIL_in_Indien.pdf

Drèze, Jean, and Amartya Sen. 2002. "India: Development and Participation." New York: Oxford University Press.

Dwivedi, O. P. 2000 "Dharmic Ecology." In *Hinduism and Ecology: The Intersection of Earth, Sky, and Water*, eds. Christopher Key Chapple, and Mary Evelyn Tucker, 3–22. Cambridge, Massachusetts.

Eckert, Julia. 2004. "Partizipation und die Politik der Gewalt: Hindunationalismus und Demokratie in Indien." *Studien zur Ethnizität, Religion und Demokratie*, Vol. 5, Baden-Baden.

FORUM for a Better Hyderabad. 2006. "Six Years of Activism and Service: Annual Number, Hyderabad: Charita Impressions." Available at: www.hyderabadgreens.org/aboutforum.html

George, Mariamma Sanu. 2006. "Non-Governmental Support System for Local Governance: Status and Possibilities." In *Decentralised Governance and Poverty Reduction: Lessons from Kerala*, eds. Balan, Ray Retna Raj, 198–217. Kerala Institute of Local Administration, Thrissur, India.

GHMC *Hyderabad City Development Plan.* Hyderabad.

Heitzman, James, and Robert L. Worden. (eds). 1995. "India: A Country Study." Washington: GPO for the Library of Congress.

HSBC. 2008. "Climate Confidence Monitor 2007." Available Online at: www.hsbc.com/1/PA_1_1_S5/content/assets/newsroom/hsbc_ccindex_p8.pdf

Harriss, John. 2005. "Middle Class Activism and Poor People Politics: An exploration of Civil Society in Chennai." Working Paper No.05-72, Working Paper Series of the Development Studies Institute of the London School of Economics, London.

Jain,B. Randhir, and P.S. Bawa. 2004. "Transparency International Country Study Report: India 2003," Transparency International, available online at: ww1.transparency.org/activities/nat_integ_systems/dnld/india.pdf

Jentsch, Gero. 2002 "Partizipation in der deutschen staatlichen Entwicklungspolitik." In *Kritische Bilanz partizipativer Ansätze in der Entwicklungszusammenarbeit.* Heinrich Böll Stiftung / HU Berlin (Seminar für ländliche Entwicklung), Entwicklungspolitische Diskussionstage 2002. online available at: www.berlinerseminar.de/bs/index.php?option=com_content&task=view&id=25&Itemid=32.

Jungk, Robert, and Norbert Müllert. 1987 "Future Workshops: How to create desirable futures." Institute for Social Interventions, London.

Kuhn, Berthold. 2006. "Möglichkeiten und Grenzen von Zivilgesellschaft in Indien." BBE Newsletter Oktober 2006. Available online at: www.b-b-e.de/uploads/media/nl2006_zivilges_indien.pdf

Lakshamanan, P. 2006. "Participatory Planning Process in Kerala." In *Decentralised Governance and Poverty Reduction: Lessons from Kerala*, eds. Balan, Ray Retna Raj, 120–129. Kerala Institute of Local Administration, Thrissur, India.

McDonnel, Ida. 2006. "Was bringt Kommunikation für Entwicklung?" *Weltnachrichten*, Vol 5/2006, Wien.

Mishra Kailash Kr. 2002. "Chaupal As Multidimensional Public Space for Civil Society in India." Paper presented in the International Seminar jointly organised by Indira Gandhi National Centre for the Arts, New Delhi and National Folklore Support Centre, Chennai in Delhi on "Folklore, Public Space and Civil Society".

Morris, Sebastian. 2002. "The Challenge to Governance in India." In *India Infrastructure Report 2002*, Indian Institute of Management Ahmedabad. Available online at: www.3inetwork.org/reports/IIR2002/chap%202.pdf

Nest, Günter. 2001. "Die raumwirksame Tätigkeit indischer Voluntary Organisations, dargestellt am Beispiel ausgewählter Landkreise (Mandals) des Bundeslandes Andhra Pradesh." Dissertation an der Fakultät VII der Technischen Universität Berlin.

Obser, Andreas. 2003. "SV Mainstreaming Participation (SVMP)", Study in the course of GTZ's sectorial plan Mainstreaming Participation. Available online at: www.gtz.de/de/dokumente/en-SVMP-obser-2003a.pdf.

Rajesh, Y.P. 2000. "Urban mismanagement blamed for killer Indian flood." Article available online at: www.planetark.org/dailynewsstory.cfm/newsid/7952/newsDate/28-Aug-2000/story.htm

Randeria, Shalini. 2004. "Verwobene Moderne: Zivilgesellschaft, Kastenbindung und nicht-staatliches Familienrecht im (post)kolonialen Indien." In *Konfigurationen zur Moderne: Diskurse zu Indien*. eds. Shalini Randeria, Martin Fuchs, and Antje Linkenbach, 155–178. Soziale Welt, Sonderband 15, Baden-Baden.

Reddy, Ratna V. 1997. "Environmental Movements in India: Some Reflections." Discussion Paper of the Research Centre for International Agrarian & Economic Development eV (FIA), 64, Heidelberg.

Reinert, Adrian, 1998. "Mobilisierung der Kompetenz von Laien: Die Methode Planungszelle/Bürgergutachten." In *Wege zur Zukunftsfähigkeit: ein Methodenhandbuch*, eds. H. Apel, D. Dernbach, Th. Ködelpeter, and P. Weinbrenner P., 115–126. Stiftung MITARBEIT, Bonn.

Schophaus, Malte, Hans-Liudger Dienel. 2003. "Die Bürgerausstellung." In *Praxis Bürgerbeteiligung: Ein Methodenhandbuch*, eds. Astrid Ley, and Ludwig Weitz, 82–90, Bonn.

Sharma, Shalendra D. 2002. "Politics and Governance in Contemporary India: The Paradox of Democratic Deepening." *Journal of International and Area Studies*, 9(1): 77–101.

Shinn, Larry D. 2000. "The Inner Logic of Gandhian Ecology." In *Hinduism and Ecology. The Intersection of Earth, Sky, and Water*. eds. Christopher Key Chapple, and Mary Evelyn Tucker, 213–241. Cambridge, Massachusetts: Harward University Press.

Society for Participatory Research in Asia. 2008. "Accessing Information under RTI: Citizens' Experiences in Ten States – 2008." New Delhi. Available online at: www.karmayog.org/rti

Srivastava, Vinay Kumar. 2006. "Religion and Environment: A Perspective from the Community of Bishnois." In *Culture, Ecology and Sustainable Development*. ed. Sukant K. Chaudhury, 195–207. New Delhi.

The Hindu. 2009. "Towards redefining living culture." Article from March 2nd, 2009. Available online at: www.thehindu.com/2009/03/02/stories/2009030258780300.htm

The Hindu. 2008. "Joint Action to improve amenities." Article from Octobre 30th, 2008. Available online at www.hindu.com/2008/10/30/stories/2008103059280300.htm

The Hindu. 2008. "'Hyderabad Unplug' day on May 3." Article from April 9th, 2008. Available online at: www.hindu.com/2008/04/09/stories/2008040958670300.htm

UNDP. 2008. "Fighting climate change: Human solidarity in a divided world." *Human Development Report 2007/2008*. New York.

Walk, Heike. 2007. "Partizipative Governance: Beteiligungsrechte und Beteiligungsformen im Mehrebenensystem der Klimapolitik", Wiesbaden.

Weber, Karsten. 2006. "Entwicklung und digitale Spaltung: Zusammenhänge und Prioritäten." *PROKLA 145 Zeitschrift für kritische Sozialwissenschaft*, 36(4), Ökonomie der Technik. Münster.

Internet Sources

http://pmindia.nic.in/Pg01-52.pdf

www.nyayabhoomi.org/treatise/history/history1.htm

www.iycn.in/about.htm

www.cgg.gov.in/cgg_home.html

http://righttoinformation.gov.in

http://203.199.178.89/apngc/index.htmas

www.pria.org

www.cwsy.org

www.goethe.de/hyderabad

www.globalcitizens.org.in/node/32

http://iycn.in/member_groups

www.hyderabadunplug.org

http://therighttowalk-kanthimathi.blogspot.com

www.hyderabadgreens.org

www.seedngo.com

www.fsdhyd.org

www.downtoearth.org.in/new_letter.asp?currentpage=1&foldername=19921031
www.save-today-survive-tomorrow.com
www.covanetwork.org
www.covanetwork.org/pucaar.htm